ODs on Finance Presents:

The Optometry Student's Guide to Financial Freedom

D1736322

Dat Bui, Aaron Neufeld
& Chris Lopez, ODs

The Optometry Student's Guide to Financial Freedom
Copyright © 2023 ODs on Finance LLC

Disclaimer:

While we are trained as doctors, we possess over two decades of combined investing experience and financial knowledge from a medical perspective. Investing inherently carries risks, including the potential loss of part or all of your investment. Any use or application of the suggestions or recommendations in this book is at your own risk, with no liability on our part. You must understand and agree to assume all risks. Neither the authors nor the publisher accept any liability for any loss or damage you may incur, including but not limited to lost profits, loss of investment, and direct, indirect, special, or consequential damages arising from your use or reliance on the information in this book.

While every effort has been made to ensure the accuracy of the information in this publication, the authors and publisher cannot be held responsible for any errors or omissions.

The content herein is for informational and educational purposes only and should not be construed as investment, financial, legal, or tax advice. If you require such advice, please consult a licensed professional.

For further information, please contact:
Email: admin@odsonfinance.com
Website: www.ODsOnFinance.com

Book and cover design by Aaron Neufeld and Dat Bui, ODs.

First Edition: October 2023

To all the optometrists who, with unwavering dedication, serve their patients with compassion and expertise on a daily basis. Your commitment not only brightens the vision of those you care for but also illuminates the path for our profession. In every eye you examine and every life you touch, you accelerate the evolution and elevation of optometry. This book is a tribute to your passion, your perseverance, and the profound impact you make every day.

CONTENTS

PROLOGUE:

THE REALITY OF OPTOMETRY: WHAT PEOPLE DON'T TELL YOU | BY AARON NEUFELD, OD

So you made your decision. You are going to optometry school. Your applications are ready, you aced the OAT (thanks Kaplan), you have a high GPA from a respectable local university, and your letters of recommendation are flawless. In fact, you had a couple extra ones that you couldn't even submit. You volunteered your weekends at a variety of clinics, participated in university research projects, and even went on a week-long medical mission trip to Haiti. Oh, and that personal statement—you're trying to be humble about it, but it definitely should win a Pulitzer Prize. All that stands in front of you are four years of intensive education and a couple of board exams. Then you're a doctor.

A doctor.

You'll have an abundance of money. More than what you will know what to do with. Life will be easy.

You'll have a large house with a view and take multiple exotic vacations per year. Fine dining, jewelry, clothes—all included in this deal. At least that's what society tells you.

Too bad society is wrong.

First, you've got that giant looming student loan over your head. Probably around $225,000, but maybe even more by the time you graduate. What's the interest on that loan? *Close to 7* *percent?* Oh, and some of the loans you took out began to accumulate interest while you were in school. Scholarships may help put a small dent in the debt, but it seems more and more insurmountable as your graduation comes around.

Then after graduation, you find a place to settle down and practice. If you find yourself in a city after graduation, you'll find that employment is hard to come by. And the harder the employment is to find, the lower your pay will be. (Damn you, supply and demand!) The boonies don't seem remotely exciting, but could they be the ticket to higher wages?

How about exam reimbursement rates? They're low and never seem to change. Vision plan companies abuse the profession of optometry on a daily basis and actively work against it. Forty dollars for an eye exam? (We're not going to name names).

Was going to school really worth it? The medical model seems a bit promising, but you often find yourself jumping through a variety of hoops. Claims rejections, scope of practice, and competing ophthalmologists who are perceived to do a "much better job than you" are just a few of these hoops.

But if that's not enough, just remember there are hundreds of thousands of individuals involved in a variety of "disruptive technologies" that are attempting to take you below the knees and reduce your profession to pure automation and mass market convenience.

Online eye exams, refraction kiosks, online optical/contact lens suppliers, and even full eye examinations done remotely are all being developed. In fact, in the near future, they will be perfected. So, yes, in addition to fellow optometrists, you will also be competing with machines. FREAKING MACHINES! Supply and demand is most definitely a cruel mistress.

Those flowers and butterflies look a lot like weeds
and mosquitos now.

Wait, It Gets Better . . . Right?

The purpose of this bleak prologue was not to depress you, but rather to give you a reality check. Graduating from optometry school is only the beginning. The truth is, optometry is not what it used to be. The so-called optometric wishing well has dried up.

Why? Well, three main factors are contributing to the ever-shrinking pot available for the eyecare industry:

1) **Decreasing/Stagnating Reimbursement Rates**

   Across the board, both vision and medical insurance are paying lower and lower amounts for optometric services and materials. What's worse, more individuals than ever are under these plans with increasingly low reimbursements. Coupled with rising inflation, higher and higher volume is required just to remain above water.

2) **Industry Saturation**

   There are simply more optometrists than there used to be. In a finite industry, this unfortunately translates to less income (on average) for each optometrist. So why are there more optometrists than ever?

   Two reasons: (A) More schools now exist with larger class sizes, and (B) fewer optometrists have a solid game plan for retirement, meaning they stay in the workforce longer[1]

---

[1] Region dependency comes into play here. We see this saturation affect urban areas much more than rural areas.

3) Desalination of Industry Capital

Disruptive technologies such as telemedicine, online refraction, subscription services, and online optical/contact lens shops are all taking from the finite capital of the industry. Couple this with corporations trying to offer heavily discounted (and often inferior) services and products, and all these desalination factors play into consumer favoritism of **convenience** and **price**, but at the cost of **quality**.

Well that was a depressing list. Does that mean you cannot be financially successful in optometry? **Absolutely not.** Plenty of us in the industry are "killing it" by being financially free and taking home large incomes that allow comfortable living. The sad part is that many of our colleagues are not. They're living paycheck to paycheck and are swallowed by massive debt. This should never be the case.

Herein lies the inspiration for writing this book. We have seen plenty of friends and colleagues at both ends of the spectrum. I remember it was around Christmastime, when Dat and I sat around a small table in a dive bar one winter evening in 2017, nursing bottled IPAs.

We talked about the usual late-twenties guy stuff: tough cases in the clinic, sports, and fast cars. when all of a sudden co-founder of ODs on Finance and co-author of this book, Dr. Dat Bui, sprung a question out of the blue:

> "I wonder how many of our colleagues are
> prepared for retirement and financially free?"

So the two of us decided to do some research. We asked

around and interviewed other optometric colleagues, and even asked other professions such as dentists, MDs, and chiropractors. **The disturbing answer?** Hardly any of these high-income professionals knew even the basics about debt, investing, or net worth. **The more disturbing news?** Many of these individuals were completely inundated with massive debt and did not realize the implications it carried for their futures.

Suddenly, a topic that we seldom talked about in the past became a passion for us. We formed the online discussion group **ODs on Finance** on Facebook. The group quickly amassed thousands of members eager to learn and explore the world of finance.

When we started running the group, we were slammed with questions. Our Facebook message inboxes were constantly spitting out new notifications. And through the various discussions we had with colleagues, we were floored by the number of ODs living life in debt, some who were many years further in their lives and careers than us.

So it got us wondering . . .

> *"How can so many doctors make financially poor decisions and fall into debt? Aren't we supposed to be smart?"*

The answer is simple. Yes, we are smart. We are smart in our craft. We are smart in diagnosing ocular disease and refracting. However, nothing about finances is taught in school. There isn't a single question on NBEO Part 1 or 2 that deals with finance.

Barring past experience in business/finance or college courses, we basically come out of optometry school being financially inept! This is, unfortunately, a recipe for disaster for someone going from making no money to making a sizable paycheck.

And that brought us to the purpose of our original book, *The Optometrist's Guide to Financial Freedom,* published in 2018, which was to give every optometrist an easy-to-read guide on how to be financially fit and savvy.

Five years later, we realized that there is something far more valuable than having a blueprint for financial success as a doctor—having one as a student!

What could be better than having all your ducks lined up in a row before you even start making a doctor's salary?

In this book we lay down a step-by-step, chapter-by-chapter guide to becoming not only financially free, but wealthy. In fact, our ultimate goal for any individual reading this book is for that individual to harness and apply the information and skills in this book.

There is absolutely no reason you cannot be debt-free and have a net worth of $1 million in five to ten years post-graduation if day in and day out you vigorously apply the principles we discuss in this book to your financial discipline.

Are you riled up? Are you ready to be prosperous? Are you ready to crush it?

We hope you said yes, because we sure are. But before we start our journey, there are a few psychological aspects we need to address:

1. Lose the Entitlement
2. Kill Your Insecurities
3. Adopt a Growth Mindset
4. Utilize Positive Projection
5. Be a Long-Term Thinker

1) Lose Your Entitlement

Nothing is owed to you when you graduate. In fact, *you* owe, and you probably owe a lot.

One thing that really grinds many seasoned ODs' gears is the entitlement of a recent graduate. (Trust us, all authors of this book had the entitlement we are about to discuss). So many new grads treat their transition from school to work as a big accomplishment. They treat themselves to a gratuitous vacation, a lavish party, a new watch, or maybe all three. They feel that they must metaphorically hold up the Lombardi Trophy, when in reality, they have not even made the practice squad.

And it's hard to blame the entitled new grad. Society places a heavy emphasis on giving praise and acclaim to those who graduate.

But what did you really accomplish? You paid a bunch of money to pass a bunch of classes and exams for four years. You were then given a piece of paper and two letters behind your name in return. This process was done by literally hundreds of thousands of people before you.

So here's the kicker. You really have not accomplished much when you graduate. But you know what the beautiful thing is? You will accomplish a lot in the future. Mentally prepare yourself to work even harder than you worked in school.

Put your passion for your career in full gear. Be humble when you start and always look forward. Consistently plan for your future and stop living in the present.

2) Kill Your Insecurities

Part of what leads to entitlement also shares a role in bringing someone to financial ruin: Insecurity.

Insecurity comes in many forms: Material insecurity ("I need that new Louis Vuitton bag!"), emotional insecurity ("Oh, they are always talking behind my back!"), and physical insecurity ("My body does not look like hers!"). More pertinent to the theme of this book are material and physical insecurity. It is easy to get caught trying to keep up with the Joneses or trying to match that Instagram or TikTok influencer *(and trust me, that Ferrari in the photo is a rental)*.

Develop a solid version of YOU. You are awesome. You will be an amazing practitioner who will help many patients. Through your work, you will become wealthy both in money and in spirit.

The most important part of killing your insecurities is being self-aware. Know yourself and your pitfalls. You will never be able to completely eliminate your insecurities, but if you know what they are, you are less likely to become a victim to them.

3) Adopt a Growth Mindset

Before we approach the actual framework of building wealth, we must first align our mindset with our goals. In her award-winning book *Mindset*, Carol Dwecker defines two types of mindsets: the fixed mindset and the growth mindset. The *fixed mindset* presents a complacent mind. It believes that it has learned all it needs to learn. It avoids anything that might result in failure, because it believes it is too good to fail. It finds learning new things and being out of its comfort zone unappealing and even offensive.

On the contrary, the *growth mindset* is a mind constantly seeking out challenges. It is not afraid to fail, because it realizes that failure is often the greatest teacher. It approaches every situation as an active learner rather than a complacent expert.

To achieve financial freedom and be the best doctor you can be, apply the growth mindset to everything you do. In no way will the journey be easy. It will present constant challenges, but the rewards will be more than worth it.

4) Utilize Positive Projection

Positive projection (first coined as one of the ten keys of closing a sale in the book *Secrets of Closing the Sale* by Zig Ziglar) is the concept of visualizing success or victory in a challenge before attempting a challenge, and then maintaining this visualization throughout the attempt at the challenge. In essence, you enter a challenge after you have already tasted the victory mentally.

Your journey out of the abyss of debt and into the throws of wealth will be riddled with pitfalls and dejection, much like your journey through final exams and practicals. You'll see pictures of friends at a music festival while you slave away on a Saturday. Your son or daughter will ask you why they cannot have a backyard pool like the neighbors. Your colleagues will wonder why you do not want to dine with them at the local Michelin star restaurant. It is important to keep your goals at the forefront of your mind. A nice dinner will give you a few hours of fun, but eliminating debt and having peace of mind financially will last a lifetime.

5) Be a Long-Term Thinker

When one builds wealth, a long-term vision must constantly be envisioned. Short-sighted thinking (no pun intended) can be deadly to your long-term financial security. Silly luxuries and temporary things often appear more appealing than your 401(k), Roth IRA, and student loan repayment. To be blunt, having the patience to pursue long-term financial goals can be brutal and unfun. Lavish living crosses every budding optometrist's mind every once in a while. But just how financially damning can short-term thinking be to you? **Let's explore the Doctor Car story.**

Dr. Typical and Dr. Mindful just graduated from optometry school with $250,000 in debt (at 7 percent interest) and land jobs that pay $120,000 a year. Let's assume they have roughly equal living expenses. Dr. Typical embodies short-term thinking, and Dr. Mindful embodies long-term thinking.

Dr. Typical immediately purchases a brand-new BMW 3 series because he now is a doctor and thus needs a "Doctor Car." The MSRP comes out to $50,000. Of course he just graduated, so he will have to make payments. He gets a favorable APR of 5 percent on five years of financing.

Dr. Mindful, on the other hand, decides to continue driving her beater. She applies the money she would have spent for the car on her student loans.

Let's explore Dr. Typical's long-term debt from his decision to be "cool." He will have to pay roughly $1,500 per month for the car, not to mention increased insurance premiums, registration, maintenance costs, and premium gasoline (add another $250 per month, give or take). That $1,500 that could have been applied to his student loan debt will continue to accrue interest.

So how does this affect Dr. Typical over the period of loan repayment? Running the numbers through the program's t-value shows that Dr. Mindful's total loan repayment amount after aggressively paying off her loan is **$267,159.90**. What about Dr. Typical's total repayment amount?: **$325,566.50**. If we take the difference between their grand totals, $58,406.60 +

$65,000 (car price + necessary attached expenses), the car actually costs a whopping $123,406.60!

That's a steep cost for a little bit of social insecurity.

When approaching financial thinking and financial security, it's important to look at the long term. Money saved now can be far more valuable than money saved later if it is invested properly. Frivolous items may appear desirable, but a life where finances are planned out and debt is never an issue is far more fulfilling and comfortable.

Your long-term approach to your finances can never occur too soon. In fact, it should be occurring even before you start your journey to becoming an optometrist.

PART I

HOW TO BE A FINANCIALLY SUCCESSFUL STUDENT

CHAPTER 1:

OPTOMETRY OR MONEY?—WHY MONEY SHOULD NOT BE YOUR PRIMARY MOTIVATOR | BY AARON NEUFELD, OD

> Success is not the key to happiness. Happiness is the key to success. If you love what you are doing, you will be successful.
> **—Albert Schweitzer**

Why did you get into optometry? This is a common question you get on your journey to becoming an OD. You undoubtedly were asked the question during your optometry school interview, and probably by many family and friends. But do not worry! If you thought you would miss being asked the question in your professional career, we can assure you that the question will pop up on at least a monthly basis—*especially in your earlier years.*

Now thinking about your answer to the question. Chances are you used the words "inspired," "passionate," and/or "service." Now imagine if you said the phrase "for the money." You would probably turn a few heads, especially those of interviewers and patients. In fact, there are probably a few jaded ODs out there who would laugh at the idea of the words "money" and "optometry" in the same sentence.

The truth is, optometry is not a financially viable profession. From a money-making standpoint, optometry is actually a horrible choice. Want proof?

A recent AOA study found that the average new grad OD (age twenty-seven) is $220,000 in debt at graduation, and that the

average employed OD (years one through five) makes an annual salary of $130,000. Consider a baseline tax rate of 35 percent on earnings. That means a net annual salary of $84,500. Now, let's say this average OD is extremely frugal and only uses $14,500/yr. to live off and contributes the remaining $70,000 to student loans. In order to reach a net worth of a whopping ZERO dollars, it would take over three years, at the age of thirty years old.

Now let's consider the alternative. At eighteen years old, the average OD foregoes going to college for work at Starbucks. Over the twelve years from age eighteen to age thirty, the prospective OD turned barista makes an average of $65,000 ($50,000 net) annually due to promotions that happen over time. Considering no debt and the same frugal living cost at $14,500/yr., that's a savings rate of $35,000 per year. Now multiply that times twelve years. **That's $420,000.** Furthermore, this is assuming that the barista stores all their savings in a savings account with no interest earnings. More than likely this number would be in the $600,000 range with proper stock/bond investing.

Thus, here are the comparative net worth of the average thirty-year-old OD and average thirty-year-old Starbucks barista, assuming similar financial/lifestyle habits:

Avg. Associate OD net worth (age thirty)	Avg. Starbucks Barista net worth (age thirty)
$0	$420,000

You didn't get in this for money.

And if you did, you did not make the greatest decision. Many other professions out there focus on making money, such as investment bankers, real estate professionals, and professional poker players.

However, just because optometry might not be the best profession for making money from a global perspective does not mean you cannot become wildly financially successful as an optometrist. Here are three factors you must consider in order to *not* myopically focus on money yet still come out a financial winner:

1) **Find Your "Thing" and Commit Your Career to Perfecting It**

   Ever wonder why specialists always make more? It's simple: they become the best at one small area/task, then build a moat around that operation, which then creates specified demand for their services, **thus allowing them to command top dollar for their services**. Your thing could be scleral contact lenses or dry eye treatment, but it could also be unique primary care in a private practice. Or it could be that you're the go-to fill-in doctor, ready to take a new challenge at the drop of a hat.

   Or it could be that you're the ultimate source of financial guidance for other ODs. (We may be a bit biased on that one.) The key is to not lose focus. Don't just work seven days to work seven days. Work because it means something to you and is building your future career, which continues to grow in value every day.

2) **Have a Solid Financial Plan from Day One**

   As you start to earn money, it's equally important to understand what to do with that money. Having a written game plan that you can refer back to helps keep you accountable for your financial goals and actions so you can better build toward a life not burdened by the need for additional income. In this book, we will be outlining various strategies for eliminating debt, building wealth through investing, and protecting those hard-earned assets.

3) **Realize That Wealth and Money Are Two Very Different Things**

   Golden handcuffs and lifestyle inflation are reported as the number one reason for physician burnout and prevent doctors from becoming truly wealthy and financially free. It's easy to fall into the cycle of lifestyle inflation as your income continues to increase. However it's important to curb the squirrel mentality (fascination for shiny things) and start the financially savvy OD mentality (fascination with debt reduction, investing, and wealth building).

You embarked on the path of optometry not for the allure of wealth, but for a deeper, more resonant call to serve and make a difference. Remember, true richness is not always measured in dollars but in the lives touched, the vision restored, and the personal fulfillment that comes from knowing you've made an impact.

Your journey in optometry can be both fulfilling and financially sound, as long as you stay true to your purpose and navigate with intention and wisdom. Embrace the challenges and rewards of your chosen path, for in them lies your unique story and legacy.

Key Takeaways:

- Based on a standard earnings time horizon, being an optometrist is technically not a wise choice. However, being financially educated can change this narrative.

- Being successful as an optometrist is rooted in three principles: finding your thing and perfecting it, having a solid financial game plan from day one, and realizing that wealth and money are two very different things.

CHAPTER 2:

HOW DOES MONEY WORK? | BY AARON NEUFELD, OD

> Too many people spend money they haven't
> earned, to buy things they don't want, to impress
> people they don't like.
> —**Will Rogers**

Money is one of the biggest topics in the world. It is constantly debated. It is attributed as the catalyst for some of the greatest successes and is also blamed as the reason for some of the biggest failures. The truth is, money makes the world run. Without money and the governmental structures that enforce its continuous use, we would be nothing but a lawless society finding sustenance and survival in the hunter-gatherer gamesmanship of our ancestors.

The reality about money is anyone can either be good or bad with finances, regardless of background. Take, for instance, the NBA star point guard who signs a contract for $10 million a year. He plays for ten years; owns cars, jets, and mansions; and throws elaborate parties. Yet five years out of retirement he finds himself bankrupt like 60 percent of his NBA peers.[2] This washed-up hoops phenomenon is a money loser; his net worth is as much as the homeless vet's sitting on the corner of the street begging for change.

Now consider your friendly neighborhood Starbucks barista

---

[2] According to a 2008 article in *The Star* about NBA players' financial security—our guess is that this statistic is probably higher today.

mentioned in chapter 1 (you know, the one that's so much wealthier than you). Through twelve-hour days of hard labor, five to six days a week, he grosses about $60,000 a year. He places half of his earnings in investment vehicles and spends frugally. After twenty years of brutal work, Mr. Barista retires as a millionaire and travels the world (while Mr. NBA star attempts to find a job bussing tables at IHOP, as he didn't have the "it factor" to work at Starbucks). Our friendly neighborhood barista is a money gainer and comes out as the winner in this story.

Now the point of this illustration is to show you that literally anyone can be horrible with finances, whether they are of a high income class or not. Consider this harrowing statistic: 78 percent of the US workforce works paycheck to paycheck. That is absolutely insane. That's doing a trampoline routine with no safety net. But consider the flipside: nearly anyone can be great with money as well.

The goal we have for you is that after finishing this book, you too will have the necessary understanding of money to achieve financial freedom. *We want you to be a money gainer.* But before we dive into the specifics of mutual funds, real estate investing, and insurance, let's first understand how money can work for us and subsequently against us. The key to understanding our fickle friend money and how to make her expand and grow lies in three vitally important concepts:

1. Income and Expenses (I/E)
2. Assets and Liabilities (A/L)
3. The IEAL Machine + IEAL Synergy

1) Income and Expenses (I/E)

If you break the word *income* apart, you'll find a simple

compound word composed of *in* and *come*. This makes sense; income describes money that is "coming in" to you. Most refer to *income* as their take-home pay. Whether it be from the check they receive every two weeks from being employed at the local VA or from the monthly distribution they take out of their private practice. While it is common to think of this direct income as the only source of income, there are actually three types of income.

The Three Types of Income:

1) Earned Income
2) Portfolio Income
3) Passive Income

Earned income or direct income is what we mentioned in the previous paragraph. It is the money you make from your day job, whether it be hourly pay or salary. Earned income is the most instantaneous of the incomes and is thought by many to be the most reliable of the incomes. However, due to these factors, earned income is also the most taxed income.

Portfolio income revolves around income made from investing in stocks, bonds, mutual funds, etc. It comprises your 401(k), IRA, and any taxable accounts you may have through entities such as Vanguard, Fidelity, etc. Portfolio income tends to be cyclical and can be volatile, as it is dependent on factors beyond an individual's control. The key term that differentiates portfolio income from earned and passive income is consistency.

Passive income involves consistent income that comes to you via investment vehicles within your control. For most individuals this will be rent collected on real estate investments. For other individuals this may include royalty payments, payments on patents, or autonomous business entities.

And now for the less sexy part: expenses. The term **expenses** encompasses anything that takes away from your income. This includes items purchased, food, rent, taxes, and nearly everything else under the sun that costs money and is either necessary or unnecessary for living.

Pitting your income against your expenses instantaneously shows your financial health. Think of it as a snapshot in the here and now. Income numbers are given a positive number, and expenses are given a negative number.

If your overall health is in the red/negative, you have *negative cash flow* and need help! This is not a sustainable lifestyle and will lead you to ruin. To get out of the red/negative and into the black/positive, you either increase the Income column (tough) or decrease the Expenses column (easier). We will have a much more in-depth look at this in our budgeting chapter. Right now, we are still just understanding how money works.

Take a look at the Instantaneous Financial Health Analyzer, aka Income/Expense Chart, below.

Are you in good financial health?

Income[3]	Expenses
• Paycheck (earned income) • Passive income	• Food • Clothing • Misc. items • Credit card monthly payment amount • Student loan monthly payment amount • Car monthly payment amount • Mortgage or rent monthly payment amount • Taxes • Real estate taxes (if applicable) • Insurance premiums—health, renters/homeowner, etc.

Assets and Liabilities

Okay, now that we have a more solid grasp on income and expenses, let's talk about assets and liabilities. No doubt you've heard the terms *assets* and *liabilities* at some point in life. While these terms are vital for judging business performance and

---

[3] Note that portfolio income is not included because it is (1) not a liquid asset (not usable right away) and 2) often stored with a target disbursement date.

profitability, they can have a more basic application to personal finance.

Assets simply represent things that give you value. This includes your house, your personal belongings, and your retirement portfolio. Quite simply, assets are things that give you monetary value. These include any real estate holding, your portfolio holdings (stocks, bonds, mutual funds, etc.) and any liquid cash you are holding.

Liabilities, on the other hand, are the antithesis of assets and incorporate things that take value away. Liabilities include student debt, credit card debt, car payments, and mortgages.

When assets and liabilities are pitted against each other on a piece of paper, this is deemed a **balance sheet**.

Assets	Liabilities
<ul><li>Real estate</li><li>Retirement portfolio</li><li>Cash in savings/checking account</li></ul>	<ul><li>Mortgage total</li><li>Student loan debt total</li><li>Credit card debt</li><li>Car loan debt total</li></ul>

Once again we can assign positive values to assets and negative values to liabilities. The difference represents your overall financial health, better known as your **net worth**.

So while income and expenses give you a value of your financial health at a current point in time, **assets and liabilities give you a better idea of your financial health over time.** To use an analogy familiar to a doctor, think of a diabetic patient— income/expenses represent blood sugar, and asset/liabilities/net worth represent A1C count. *(If this isn't ringing a bell, pick up your physiology textbook and get some remedial studying in!)*

Income/Expenses and Assets/Liabilities Synergy

Okay, so at this point you're probably thinking, "Well, now I understand how assets, liabilities, income, and expenses relate to me, but how do I get my net worth to seven digits and beyond? What gives?"

Relax a bit and take a step back.

Now that we have our basic concepts, let's see how we can relate them to real-world transactions. Let's explore how these four terms work synergistically, either very much for you or very much against you. Much like when you learned to treat glaucoma, you first needed to learn *(1) the different parts of the eye followed by (2) the physiology of the eye and its relation to the optic nerve, and (3) the methods of treating glaucoma.* Our definitions above represent the anatomy; now let's jump into the physiology and explore the synergy of these concepts. Once we understand the synergy, we can then understand how to manipulate this synergy in our favor.

First, let's burn this image into our brains:

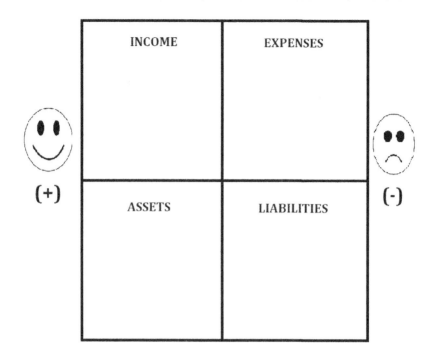

This will be our diagram of our four concepts working together. This four-headed synergistic beast, which we will now lovingly refer to as the IEAL machine (because we want to be super original here—does sarcasm convey well over text?) can be found working in two different environments:

1) **Self vs. Debt Collector**

2) **Self vs. Debt Ower**

Alright, let's go a little deeper.

Self vs. Debt Collector

Let's say you just got your very first paycheck as an employed optometrist. (Go you!) You are feeling awesome and decide to take all your friends out for drinks. You buy everyone a few rounds because, hey, you're freaking awesome and liquid courage is really speaking to you. The total bill is $500 when everyone decides to leave the bar. Let's send this through the IEAL machine.

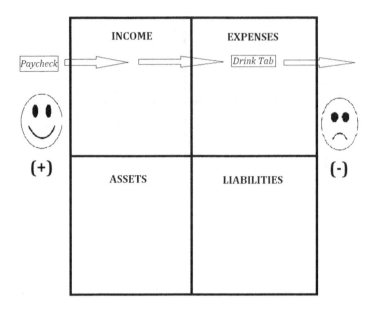

Pretty simple. Money goes into your account, you purchase a product (in this case forty-five shots of Patron or ninety-two pints of Coors Light), and money goes out of your account. Let's say you decide to use a credit card to make your purchase rather than cash, which was assumed in the previous schematic. Let's run the IEAL machine again:

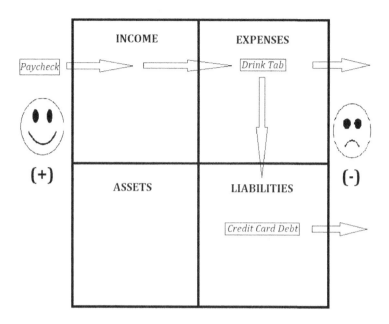

Now we can see that instead of an immediate expense, the credit card debt incurred by the purchase now turns it into a liability. Keep in mind that the expense still exists, because you will have to pay for the expense at some time. The difference now is that that expense could possibly be more if you let your credit card debt sit and let interest pile on it.

Obviously, placing a large bar tab on your credit card affects both your financial health and net worth (remember: income/expenses relate to immediate financial health, and assets/liabilities relate to net worth) in a negative way. But much like the first law of thermodynamics, which states that energy cannot be created or destroyed in a closed system, so too does the same principle apply to money in a transaction. So who benefits from your incurred alcohol debt?

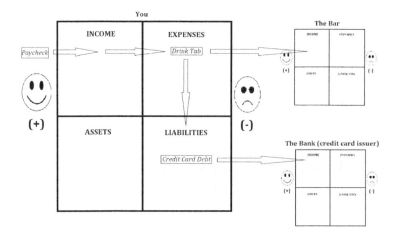

Hope you're not having flashbacks from ray-tracing exams in first-year Optics class! But as you can see, your hard-earned money goes to two debt collectors, the bar and the bank. What you see right above you is the **cycle of consumerism**. This is the reason that businesses flourish, people are employed, and housing/stock prices go up. **Why?** Because if we expanded this schematic further, we would see that under "The Bar's" and "The Bank's" Expenses component, there would be Employee Payroll (mind blown? You're welcome).

This cycle of consumerism is also how most people view the only way to use money. Sadly, it is the reason why 78 percent of America lives paycheck to paycheck. They cannot get out of the cycle of consumerism. They hemorrhage money at a rate at which it is impossible to keep more than they spend. The 78 percent is like a collective hamster stuck running in a spinning wheel that goes nowhere.

Well, you don't have to be that hamster. It's time to break out of that cage and run free.

But how? The solution is brutally simple: reverse the cycle.

Self vs. Debt Ower

That's right. Instead of owing the debts, be the one who issues the debts. Sure, throughout life you will always have debts in the form of expenses and liabilities. But if you can get your money to work for you, you can turn back the cycle so your income and assets continually rise while your expenses and liabilities continually fall. When you get to a level where the income your assets generate can support you, you've reached financial freedom. Or as they call it in the streets, being rich.

The process cannot happen overnight. In fact, it takes a lot of time and even more patience. Assets such as stock/bond holdings, businesses you own, and real estate investments can help tip the cycle heavily in reverse, and subsequently, heavily in your favor.

Say, for instance, you buy some real estate, a two-bedroom condo that you rent out to a nice couple. Let's compare their IEAL machine to your IEAL machine:

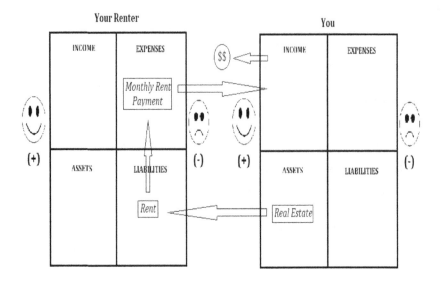

Look at how much better that is than our previous example of grabbing watered-down tequila in a dive bar! You could run a similar model if you own a practice or other business entity. Just replace "monthly rent payment" with "materials" or "services."

Financial Independence, with the Option of Retiring Early (FIRE)

There is a good chance you have heard of the FIRE movement, as it has become increasingly popular. FIRE is an acronym that stands for Financial Independence Retire Early. While we might not necessarily want to retire early, having financial independence enables us to take that path and have that peace of mind if needed.

Ultimately, financial independence means that an individual no longer needs to rely on their nine-to-five job to supply the income needed for survival.

Rather, they can turn to the assets that were built up through meticulous saving and planning to support them and their family.

What this chapter serves as is a primer for your approach to money. When you get your paycheck, think of that money as something that can grow and create more money. Think of the IEAL machine whenever you get tempted by a large purchase (or even a small purchase). Most unneeded material items (e.g., jewelry, clothes, etc.) and fleeting purchases (e.g., lavish, unneeded vacations) are sunk costs that increase not only your expenses, but also your liabilities. Always find ways to fill the Assets component of your IEAL machine. You will continually generate income and set yourself on a course for financial freedom.

Key Takeaways:

- Anyone can be good or bad with finances—it comes down to your education and discipline around money.

- Understand the IEAL (income, expenses, assets, liabilities) machine. Realize that the worldview of being on the right side of the machine will lead to a lifetime of catching up, while being on the left side of the machine will allow you to reach financial freedom.

CHAPTER 3:

HOW TO PAY FOR SCHOOL | BY DAT BUI, OD

*An investment in knowledge pays the best
interest.*
—Benjamin Franklin

After receiving your formal admission letter and selecting your school of choice, more than likely at some point you may have asked yourself, "How in the world am I going to pay for the next four years of my education?"

If you did ask yourself this, you're not alone. On average, optometry school by itself can cost upward of $150,000–$250,000. Factor in living costs, loan interest, and the four years of refractive and ocular health knowledge, and it can balloon to a total cost of $300,000–$400,000 easily!

So how do we find this large six-figure sum of cash to pay for that priceless education and degree? It really comes down to five main ways:

1. **Pay with Cash**
2. **Pay with Scholarships or Get a Discount**
3. **Work While in School**
4. **Use Federal Forgiveness Programs**
5. **Take Out Student Loans**

1) Pay with Cash

A few optometry students land in the very fortunate position of being able to pay for their education with cash. This may be from an inheritance, some sort of prize money or through the graces of a benevolent parent or family member. **If you have the money upfront to pay for school, then most traditional knowledge says you should do so.** Sure, you could invest that money and hope that it beats out loan interest, but remember that loan interest is one of the only guaranteed returns (since there is no change in interest rate)—whereas all other investments like stocks or BTCs do not have a necessarily guaranteed return.

529 or Education Saving Accounts Plans (ESA)

Even if you do not have the cash to pay for the entire education, check if you have any savings in a dedicated education account such as a 529 or Education Saving Account (ESA). This might have been set up by your parents or grandparents to help fund your higher education. It is wise to use all remaining funds in these accounts!

Retirement Accounts (IRAs, 401K)

Next, If you have retirement account money in an Individual Retirement Account (IRA), Roth IRA, 401(k), or similar account, **I generally advise against tapping that to pay for your education.** Since that money is both tax protected and asset protected, it is best to leave it compounding for retirement in the future. But if you choose to use that money for your education, there are a few special rules that you have to be aware of or risk a heavy tax penalty.

The general rule with retirement accounts is **you can always withdraw as much as you want from a retirement account.**

However, if you withdraw money from the account prior to age 59 1/2, you will owe a 10 percent penalty on the withdrawal, in addition to the taxes that would be due on withdrawals from a tax-deferred account. College or professional school costs are an exception to that 10 percent penalty, at least up to the amount of the legitimate educational expenses, but only for IRAs, not 401(k)s.

If you choose to go this route for funding your school, make sure to roll over all your existing 401(k) money to a Roth IRA first. This will trigger a tax event, but since you have no significant earned income as a student, your tax bill will likely be zero.

A Roth IRA is an account that is not subject to taxes, primarily intended for retirement purposes. If you decide to withdraw money from the account for educational expenses, you may be liable to pay taxes on any earnings withdrawn. Nonetheless, the account permits you to first withdraw the initial amount you contributed, which is tax-free. If you withdraw all of the contributed amount and then proceed to withdraw earnings, those earnings can also be tax-free if used for education. However, this is only applicable if at least five tax years have passed since you made your first contribution to an IRA. This requirement may pose a challenge for many optometry students during their initial year of school, but it becomes less restrictive as they progress through their education.

It's important to clarify that **student loan funds cannot be used to contribute to retirement accounts such as IRAs**. Only income that has been earned from a work-study job, for example, is eligible for retirement account contributions.

If you find yourself unfamiliar with the terms mentioned in the preceding paragraphs, fear not. We will delve into these concepts in the retirement section later in the book.

Overall, we do NOT recommend tapping into retirement funds to fund your education. Let that compounding growth work its magic, so after four years of school, you will have a fairly decent chunk of investment.

Family Loans

When it comes to receiving financial assistance from family members for optometry school, it's important to approach the situation with careful consideration. If the assistance is in the form of a gift, then expressing gratitude and accepting it can be straightforward. However, if it is a loan, a more thorough evaluation is necessary, as owing money to a family member can create complicated dynamics.

First, it is essential to ensure that any loan from a family member is legal and properly documented. **Draft a simple promissory note that outlines key details, such as the interest rate calculation, payment terms, due dates, prepayment options, and conditions for loan forgiveness.** Keep in mind that the IRS requires family loans to charge a minimum interest rate, which varies annually based on the loan's duration. Interest rates can be as low as 0.18% for short-term loans and 1.01% for long-term loans.

Any interest that is not charged may be considered a gift for tax purposes. As long as the amount falls below the annual gift tax limit (e.g., $17,000 in 2023), it typically does not pose a problem. If the forgiven interest exceeds the gift tax limit, a gift tax return may need to be filed.

Family lenders residing outside the US should also review their local tax laws for similar regulations.

Parents sometimes opt to borrow money for their child's education using methods such as federal Parent PLUS Loans, private student loans, home equity lines of credit (HELOCs), or credit cards. However, it is generally advisable for the student to be the borrower on the loan. This allows them to have a vested interest in their education, take advantage of federal forgiveness or income-driven repayment programs, and have the ability to discharge the debt in the event of death or permanent disability.

If you do borrow money from family, it is crucial to safeguard their interests by obtaining adequate term life and disability insurance as soon as possible. This ensures that they won't face financial burdens if something unexpected happens to you. Don't worry, we will discuss this in further detail in later chapters.

Additionally, it's important to carefully consider the financial stability of the family member offering the loan or gift. As a responsible optometry student, you will eventually have the future earning means to repay your education expenses. However, it's crucial to ensure that accepting financial support doesn't compromise your family's retirement savings or mortgage obligations. Each family and cultural context is unique, so navigate these decisions based on your personal circumstances. Generally, prioritizing parental financial independence and retirement should be paramount.

Remember, mixing money with family can often cause unnecessary stress and subconscious obligations. Christmas dinner sitting across the table from your uncle who you owe money to can taste quite different.

2) Pay with Scholarships/Get a Discount

Scholarships are a great way to lighten the load of school costs. They can be a result of academic achievement, community involvement, leadership recognition, future work, or demographic relation. Rarely do scholarships cover the entirety of school costs (there are no NCAA basketball full rides, despite what your school's intramural league says); however, there are exceptions. Let's go over a few different types of scholarships available to optometry students.

WICHE (Western Interstate Commission for Higher Education)

There are some optometry schools that allow you to pay state resident tuition despite coming from out of state, such as UC Berkeley or SUNY (at least after the first year). Definitely check with school admissions prior to applying.

Another great program is the **WICHE (Western Interstate Commission for Higher Education) program for optometrists,** which is a regional program in the United States that aims to address the shortage of optometrists in certain states within the Western region. The program facilitates the exchange of students between participating states, allowing residents of one state to attend optometry schools in other participating states at reduced tuition rates.

Through the WICHE program, qualified residents of participating states can enroll in out-of-state optometry programs and pay a reduced tuition rate comparable to the in-state tuition of the host state. This program helps expand access to optometric education for students who may not have optometry schools in their home states or who wish to pursue specialized programs not available locally.

As of 2023, if you are a resident of the following states, you can apply for the WICHE program up to $20,575 annually during the four years of optometry school.

- Alaska
- Arizona
- Colorado
- Hawaii
- Montana
- New Mexico
- North Dakota
- Utah
- Wyoming

Please read the fine print, as most optometrists are required to practice back in their resident states post-doctorate for a specific number of years (usually four years).

Military Health Professions Scholarship Programs

The military offers a program known as the Health Professions Scholarship Program (HPSP), which is commonly used to finance doctorate education. A lot of my fellow classmates personally utilized this method to fund their schooling, but I believe the program is mislabeled as a scholarship. It should be regarded as a contract rather than a traditional scholarship. Under this program, the military covers your tuition, fees, and required expenses while also providing a taxable living stipend, which was approximately $2,200 per month in 2023. In return for these generous benefits, you are obligated to serve the military for a year of active duty as a practicing professional for each year you received the scholarship.

It is important to note that **military optometrists often receive significantly lower pay compared to their civilian counterparts**. Furthermore, the military governs various aspects of your professional and personal life, including the location of your base when not deployed, the duration and location of your deployments to war zones, working hours, colleagues, dress code (usually a military uniform), and more.

From a financial standpoint, the HPSP scholarship can be more advantageous if you attend an expensive optometry school. However, many doctors find that the financial outcomes are similar regardless of whether they utilize the HPSP scholarship or pay for school through other means, such as taking a high-paying rural position for two to three years. With the HPSP, you receive more upfront funding from the military but may have less income later on. **Therefore, the primary consideration in deciding whether to pursue the HPSP scholarship to pay for optometry school should be your desire to serve as a military doctor,** at least during the initial phase of your career. If you do aspire to become a military doctor, the HPSP can be one of the best ways to finance your education. However, if a military medical career is not your goal, it is advisable to avoid this path, as signing up primarily for financial reasons can lead to significant challenges and dissatisfaction.

I understand that the previous paragraphs may have presented military service and the HPSP scholarship in a less favorable light. However, I believe it is crucial to present the facts about how the program works transparently, as it benefits not only individuals but also the military. While being in the military has provided many of my OD buddies with numerous positive experiences and there are many admirable aspects of military practice and serving one's country—it is important to consider the frequent changes associated with military service.

Therefore, it would be wise for any prospective HPSP applicant, especially those without prior active duty experience, to personally speak with several current active-duty optometrists, including individuals who regret their decision to join, before accepting the scholarship.

Indian Health Service (IHS)

Indian Health Services (IHS) operates a program that can be referred to as a "scholarship" but is essentially a contractual arrangement for optometry students. To be eligible for this program, you must be a member of a federally recognized American Indian tribe or Alaska Native village. The program offers a taxable monthly living stipend of at least $1,500 and covers all tuition and fees associated with your optometry education. In return for receiving the scholarship, you are required to commit to one year of service for each year of scholarship support, with a minimum commitment of two years. Your service must be fulfilled at a designated Indian Health Service facility or another practice where at least 75 percent of the patient population consists of Native Americans.

Corporate Employer Loan Repayment Programs

Certain private employers in the optometry field, such as LensCrafters or Walmart Optometry, may offer loan repayment programs as part of their benefits package. These programs typically cover a portion of the optometry student's tuition expenses and can last anywhere from two to four years. It's important to note that this benefit is usually taxable, although recent legislation has made a portion of it tax-free for the employee while remaining tax-deductible for the employer.

It's worth considering that employers often view loan repayment programs as an alternative to providing a higher salary, rather than an additional benefit on top of the salary. Nevertheless, it can serve as an additional point of negotiation when you are seeking your first job after completing your optometry training. These programs often come with certain requirements, such as working in specific locations within the United States, particularly in more rural areas.

3) Work While in School

Another way to pay for school is to actively work while in school and put that money toward loans. Remember that while you are a full-time student, there are a lot of work-study jobs available either on campus or in the clinic. While many of these part-time gigs don't pay much, they do offer flexibility as a student, and they are even better if they allow you some downtime to study while on the job.

Also, working at a private practice on weekends is a great way to gain some extra cash and get networking opportunities with potential future employers. But remember, working while in school should be approached with caution and proper perspective. Sure, extra money is great, but remember that your biggest priority is your education.

4) Federal Forgiveness Program

Public Service Loan Forgiveness (10 years PSLF)

The Public Service Loan Forgiveness (PSLF) program is a popular method for optometry students to finance their education, especially if you plan to work for an academic university or non-profit such as the Veterans Affairs (VA) or Indian Health Services (IHS). Under this program, eligible students who make 120 on-time monthly payments on qualifying federal direct loans through federal Income-Driven Repayment (IDR) programs while working full time for a qualifying federal, state, or non-profit 501(c)(3) employer can have any remaining debt forgiven tax-free, usually after ten years. The PSLF program was officially launched in 2007, and the first cohort of eligible borrowers became eligible for forgiveness in 2017. However, due to various reasons, only a small number of doctors are expected to receive forgiveness before 2021–2023. As time passes, more borrowers have a higher rate of success qualifying for forgiveness each year due to legislative provisions to the program.

The PSLF program is particularly beneficial for doctors with a significant federal student loan burden who have spent an extended period in residency and plan to pursue an academic career, at least for the initial years after training. During residency, payments through IDR programs can be as low as $0 per month while still counting toward the required 120 payments. As a result, an optometrist who completes one year of residency and maybe another two additional years of fellowship may only need to make substantial payments for seven years before the remaining balance, **potentially amounting to hundreds of thousands of dollars**, is forgiven tax-free.

If you choose the PSLF program as your method of financing optometry school, it is crucial to maintain meticulous records of every qualifying payment made and retain your annual employer certification forms. It is essential to fill out the application accurately. In the first year of possible forgiveness (2017), a significant number of applicants (99 percent) were rejected. While many were deemed ineligible due to various reasons (such as having ineligible loans, using an ineligible loan program, or working for an ineligible employer), a noteworthy percentage faced rejection simply because they failed to complete the application correctly. Obtaining forgiveness may require persistence, as the government and loan servicing companies representing the government may not readily grant it. It is recommended that you consult with a student loan specialist to ensure you are meeting the requirements.

Income-Driven Repayment Forgiveness Program (20 to 25 years)

The Income-Driven Repayment (IDR) programs offer their own forgiveness options that do not necessitate full-time employment with a 501(c)(3) or government employer. However, these programs have significant drawbacks. First, they require borrowers to make payments for twenty to twenty-five years, a longer duration compared to the ten-year requirement of other forgiveness programs. Most optometrists will likely have fully repaid their loans within that time frame, even while making minimum payments. Secondly, the forgiveness obtained through IDR programs is considered taxable income at the recipient's ordinary income tax rates in the year it is received. **For individuals with a substantial debt-to-income ratio, this tax obligation, often referred to as a "tax bomb," can exceed the original loan amount.**

These disadvantages render these programs unappealing to the majority of borrowers. However, there are specific cases where IDR programs may be viable, primarily for individuals with **exceptionally high debt-to-income ratios** who are unable to secure or unwilling to pursue employment that qualifies for Public Service Loan Forgiveness (PSLF).

Don't worry, we will cover these forgiveness programs more in detail in **chapter 14, "Preparing for Student Loan Debt After Graduation"**—but the general advice is NOT to pursue these programs until after you are done with optometry school. You won't know what type of optometric modality you will like! You might take out a massive amount in student loans, betting that you will just work for a VA for ten years post-graduation to get it forgiven, only to find you dread working there!

Lastly, yes, we do NOT recommend going for an Income-Driven **Repayment Forgiveness Program (twenty to twenty-five years) unless it is absolutely necessary.** Heck, by reading this book, you will be so financially prepared you won't even have to think about going that desperate route.

5) Take Out Student Loans

If you're like 95 percent of optometry students, then you will probably take out student loans to pay for school, and there's nothing wrong with that! Rarely does anyone have a quarter or half million dollars just sitting around ready to be used for their education.

Student loans serve as a proverbial double-edged sword for most optometry students. On one hand, they give you the means and ability to fund your education and future, but on the other hand, they have the ability to be extremely costly and grab a stranglehold on your future finances.

Student loans are an immense point of stress, but they don't have to be! We will give you a thorough breakdown on how to manage and tackle your student loans in chapter 14.

The key takeaway is that while student loans are a necessary investment in your earning potential, your goal is to take out as little as possible and live like a broke/frugal student!

Key Takeaways:

- If you have the financial means, paying for optometry education upfront with cash is often recommended due to the guaranteed return of avoiding loan interest. Additionally, consider utilizing any existing funds in dedicated education accounts, such as 529 or Education Saving Accounts (ESA), that may have been established by your family to support your higher education.

- Avoid tapping your retirement accounts (IRA, 401[k]) to fund your education. Let it continue to work its compounding magic and grow.

- There are a lot of scholarships and repayment programs available, but be cautious since many of these programs require career commitment post-graduation. So read the fine print!

- Working while in school, even one day a week, is a great way to cover some of your expenses.

- While there are federal forgiveness programs available, like the ten-year PSLF, don't rely on this route until you have a clearer idea of which modality you enjoy practicing in. We do not recommend relying on an Income-Driven Repayment Forgiveness Program (twenty to twenty-five years).

CHAPTER 4:

HOW TO SAVE MONEY IN OPTOMETRY SCHOOL | BY AARON NEUFELD, OD

Do not save what is left after spending, but spend what is left after saving.
—Warren Buffett

Optometry school encompasses four years of your life where you will gain a plethora of knowledge that you will utilize for the rest of your life. It will be a time where you gain intangible skills, but a time where you will not gain money.

In fact, you'll be losing money at an alarming rate. Consider this: at the time that this book is published, the average optometry school tuition for four years runs roughly $250,000. Furthermore, consider that the average optometry student's living expenses for four years equate to about $100,000. Broken down yearly, that's about $87,500. Broken down daily, that's $239.72.

Yes, let that sink in. Being in optometry means you are losing $239.72 PER DAY.

While the majority of your earnings to offset that unfortunate daily burden happen after you graduate, there are a few strategies you can utilize to minimize the effects of this negative cash flow and later debt burden while you are in school.

1. Obtain Scholarships

Scholarships come in many varieties and can range wildly in dollar value, as noted in detail in the previous chapter.

Ask around at your school and research online to find out about opportunities and apply for as many as possible. If you think this is too much work, remember your negative cash flow (~$239.72 per day), and then think about the time it would take you to apply for the scholarship and the possible reward that can offset that daily negative cash flow.

2. Limiting Loans

One of the most alarming aspects of student loans is just how easy they are to get. Many times, students can get lured into the trap of opening Pandora's "free money box." Remember that loan money is by no means free and will cost you quite a bit in the future. So make sure to utilize only the bare minimum of loan money possible while in school. If you have savings in the bank, try to use it first before pulling out additional loans.

Whenever possible, try to avoid private loans (which often have higher interest rates). Most students can maximize their use of direct federal loans (typically at lower rates), which are more than sufficient to cover their expenses. Furthermore, federal loans are the only ones eligible for Income-Driven Repayment (IDR) and Public Service Loan Forgiveness (PSLF) programs, should you ever need them. If you must take out private loans, such as in a true life emergency, borrow as little as possible.

If you must take additional loan money, make sure to compare interest rates if you have different options.

3. Limiting Equipment Purchases

Equipment purchases have become a mainstay in optometry school. Many equipment companies create partnerships with schools in an effort to familiarize students with their product line in hopes of creating lifelong customers. Schools will often lump equipment purchasing in with textbook purchasing; however, you as the student (ahem, consumer) should have the power to tell your school which pieces of equipment you actually want to purchase.

Purchasing equipment during optometry school can be financially damning for three reasons:

1. More than likely, it will be purchased with loan money.
2. It will be purchased new, at full price.
3. It will go through depreciation and have lesser resale value after school.

So what's the solution? Look for used equipment or opportunities to borrow, and only purchase essential items. While a retinoscope, 90D/78D/20D lens, and BIO are mainstays for standard-of-care practicing, items such as a lens clock and MIO are not and should be avoided.

4. Working Part Time

Another way to counteract negative cash flow (remember the sobering number of ~$239.72 per day, lest you forget!) is by attacking it with positive cash flow. This comes in the form of earning money.

Part-time work can take three different forms for optometry students:

1) **Federal work-study (FWS) programs**—allow students with financial need to obtain jobs allocated within the school to pay for their education. Commonly, these jobs include being a library assistant, lab TA, or operations assistant.

2) **Employed (W2) job**—such as working as a tech for an

optometry office or working a more standard job like a waiter or cashier.

3) **Independent contractor (1099) job**—such as tutoring, teaching, or helping out in a non-regular/scheduled manner. Sometimes these jobs pay under the table.

A quick note on working part time: it is not for everyone. Understand your limitations, prioritize studying for classes and boards, and absolutely do not let it take priority over your schooling.

A personal cautionary anecdote

I remember an individual in a class above me when I was in optometry school. He had two jobs and drove a brand-new Dodge Charger. He would always tell us how much cash he was making each week. This poor individual unfortunately had to repeat his third year not once, but three times. On the third time, he was given an ultimatum from our dean that if he did not pass he would be expelled. He was expelled and now works as an assistant manager at a fitness center, saddled with seven years of optometry school debt.

Taking an additional year to graduate is one of the costliest decisions a student can make. Whether due to a gap year prior, academic challenges, or NBEO retakes (remember that Part 1 NBEO has only a 60 percent passing rate), it all has a financial impact. You will need to cover living expenses, and there may be additional tuition fees. However, the most significant expense is the opportunity cost of *forgoing a year of earning a doctor's salary during your career.* Considering it from this perspective, it becomes clear that taking a gap year should only be pursued if the benefits outweigh the financial consequences.

Remember balance, and remember that the bigger paychecks come after school is completed.

5) Understand the Cost of and Budget for Board Exams

It's no secret, taking NBEO Part I, II and III is expensive (at the time of publication of this book in 2023, each part costs $1380 to take). Test preparation courses are also expensive. In fact, if a student were to take all three parts of boards and pass on the first try with the help of prep courses, they could be looking at a total bill of over $10,000!

So how do you pass boards in the most financially responsible way possible?

1) **Make sure you pass the first time**—Sure, it's a bit of an obvious statement, but board studying should hold serious gravity on your lifestyle for the months leading up to the big tests. Focus heavily on passing, so you can forever put it behind you.

2) **Find the test prep route that is right for you**—While most optometrists utilize one or two of the test prep companies out there to pass boards, not every optometrist necessarily needs to utilize one, all, or any test-prep course! Analyze how you learn best and see which route can help you the most.

Saving money while in optometry school is akin to mastering a complex visual field test; it demands attention to detail, discernment, and the application of learned strategies. By proactively managing your expenses, seeking financial opportunities, and making informed decisions, you pave the way for a sustainable and financially positive future.

Key Takeaways:

- On average, you are losing nearly $250 PER DAY while you are in optometry school, so saving money is of paramount importance!

- Limit equipment purchases and taking out additional loans, while offsetting costs with scholarships and working.

- Remember that the most expensive things you can do in optometry school are (1) retake a year (not only because of extra loans, but also because of a year of income lost) and (2) retake an NBEO exam.

CHAPTER 5:

HOW TO LIVE FRUGALLY & THE IMPORTANCE OF A BUDGET | BY DAT BUI, OD

A budget isn't about restricting what you can spend. It gives you permission to spend without guilt or regret.
—Dave Ramsey

"It is easy to be broke as a student when everyone else around you is also broke!" That saying cannot be more true while you are in optometry school. Frugality is a critical financial principle for just about anyone, but it is particularly important for students who will spend most of their twenties in school.

While both *cheap* and *frugal* involve spending money wisely, there is a subtle difference in their connotations and approaches to financial matters, leading to a societal misconception. **Being** *cheap* **typically refers to a mindset focused solely on spending as little money as possible**, often prioritizing short-term savings over long-term value or quality. Cheap individuals tend to seek the lowest price at any cost, sometimes compromising on quality or denying themselves reasonable comforts. They may prioritize immediate savings over considering the potential long-term consequences or value of their purchases. Often they take advantage of other people's generosity and cause stress to people around them.

On the other hand**, being** *frugal* **implies a more strategic and mindful approach to spending.**

Frugal individuals seek value for their money by carefully

considering their purchases and making intentional choices. They aim to maximize the utility and longevity of their purchases while minimizing wastefulness. Frugality often involves finding ways to save money without sacrificing quality or essential needs. It emphasizes long-term financial health and sustainability.

So the key to financial freedom is living a mindful & frugal life.

As an optometry student, it is crucial to live within your means or even *below* your means in order to leverage student loan debt interest in your favor rather than against you. When you finance your education through debt, you are essentially living above your means and accumulating increasing debt each month.

Minimizing the amount of debt you accumulate while in school is paramount to your financial well-being. After selecting a school, the most effective way to achieve this is by practicing frugality during your four years as a student.

Let's consider an example: If you borrow $100 at 8 percent interest during your first year of optometry school, and the interest compounds over four years of study and is paid off over twenty years, that initial $100 will accrue 8 percent compound interest for nearly three decades. At an 8 percent interest rate, that $100 will have grown to over $1,000. **Essentially, whatever you purchase with those initial borrowed dollars will end up costing you ten times the original price.**

While a more realistic scenario may involve a fifteen-year repayment period with an average interest rate of 6 percent, even then, you will be paying 2.5 times the sticker price for items bought with borrowed money. Every computer, meal out, car, or bus pass will cost 2.5 times more than you initially think when you finance it through debt as an optometry student.

These numbers highlight the importance of keeping your student debt burden low. Although a high income may await you in the future, matching it with a substantial debt burden will require a significant portion of your doctor's salary to service that debt. By making wise and frugal spending choices now, you will thank yourself in the future.

How to Budget Effectively as a Student:

I know that budgeting is not fun, but it is vital to see where your money is going and control your spending, and thus the amount of student loans you need to take out. Every student should budget for a minimum of three months to know exactly how much they actually **NEED** for necessary expenses (such as rent/utilities) vs. **WANT** (such as that Beyoncé concert ticket). Once you identify the difference, you can really spend money on what really brings you joy!

A free tool that I recommend is **Mint's Budgeting App** to track your spending. You will be shocked by how much you actually spend each month. Don't worry, it will usually take you two to three months to get it down within a few dollars! So be flexible during this transition period.

Here is a typical budget that I recommend for students:

Monthly Budget			
Categories	Needs vs. wants	Budget allowance	Actual spent
Tuition/textbooks/clinical equipment	Needs	$4,100 (varies)	
Rent (single room) with housemates	Needs	$600	
Utilities (shared)	Needs	$50	
Cell phone bill	Needs	$75	
Groceries	Needs	$150	
Home supplies	Needs	$50	
Personal care	Needs	$100	
Car insurance/ maintenance	Needs	$120	
Gas/fuel	Needs	$100	
Netflix	Wants	$10	

Music (spotify)	Wants	$10	
Coffee/drinks	Wants	$25	
Restaurant, dining out & fast food	Wants	$150	
Entertainment (anything that bring you joy, like concerts, bar tab, gifts to families/friends)	Wants	$150	
	Total	$5,190	

Financial Tip

If you hate budgeting, do a **reverse budget** where you allocate all funds FIRST into your required bills such as rent, student loan debt, retirement and/or short-term investing goals, then spend whatever is left over, GUILT-FREE

On a more personal note, I found out a few personal things about myself while living on a strict budget, such as what actually brings true joy to my life. In my early twenties, going out to bars/clubs with my buddies was often the highlight of my week. But when I started to budget and I had less money to spend, I realized that just being around my loved ones was the true joy. We didn't need to drop $200 a night on bottle service to enjoy each other's company, when a simple board game night was enough.

In addition, because I had a set fund every month, **I really had to prioritize goals and/or people that were really important in my life.** If it was my little nephew's birthday that month, I would say no to a friend's dinner because I would have to sacrifice some of my restaurant allowance to save up for it.

Another reason to embrace frugal living in optometry school lies in the realm of **behavioral finance**. It is easier to increase your standard of living than to decrease it. This phenomenon, known as **lifestyle inflation**, often leads to spending more without a permanent increase in happiness. Surprisingly, many small increases in spending tend to bring more joy than a single large increase.

By practicing frugality as a student, even modest improvements in lifestyle during your doctor career will feel like indulgences and bring greater satisfaction. If you can maintain a "live like a broke student" mentality for the first five years post-graduation while accumulating a doctor's salary, your path to wealth building will be significantly accelerated.

Key Takeaways:

- Frugality is crucial for optometry students—live within or below your means and leverage interest in your favor.

- Being cheap involves prioritizing short-term savings without considering long-term value or quality, while being frugal entails making strategic and mindful spending choices to maximize value and minimize wastefulness.

- Minimizing debt accumulation is vital for financial well-being, as borrowed money accrues compound interest over time, resulting in significantly higher costs.

- Taking an additional year to graduate can be financially costly due to expenses, tuition fees, and the opportunity cost of delaying earning a doctor's salary.

- Optometry students are advised to minimize private loans and prioritize direct federal loans, which offer lower interest rates and eligibility for repayment programs.

- Budgeting is important to see where every single dollar goes and reduce the overall spending.

- Embracing frugal living helps avoid lifestyle inflation and allows for a faster path to wealth building by maintaining a "live like a broke student" mentality.

CHAPTER 6:

HOW TO AVOID FINANCIAL CATASTROPHE THAT YOU CANNOT INSURE AGAINST | BY DAT BUI, OD

It's not the strongest of the species that survive, nor the most intelligent, but the one most responsive to change.
—Charles Darwin

Insurance is often the last thing anyone will think about when it comes to finances. Too many people, including doctors, only buy insurance to protect against a financial loss that is not a true financial catastrophe—for example, AppleCare for their iPhone or a warranty for their TV—meanwhile, they do not bother to purchase term life or disability insurance.

So first, let's define what true financial catastrophes are. Financial catastrophes have the potential to significantly impede your progress toward achieving your financial goals, often causing setbacks that may last for years or even decades. Numerous instances of such catastrophes exist, varying in their insurability. While certain financial catastrophes can be safeguarded against through insurance, others unfortunately cannot.

Financial catastrophes that you CANNOT insure against:

- Failure to graduate optometric program
- Failure to pass the NBEO exams
- Career change from optometry
- Divorce

- Gambling and/or drug addiction
- Loss of professional license (malpractice)

In this chapter, we are going to focus on the *uninsurable financial catastrophes,* and we will discuss insurance (mainly life and disability) in the next chapter.

1. Failure to Graduate Optometric Program and/or Pass NBEO Exams

It seems that more and more optometry schools are popping up every year, and optometric admissions are putting less and less weight on academic credentials, such as science GPA and OAT scores. The trend we have been noticing lately is that rather than looking for the most academically qualified, the schools' goals are to find students who are academically okay but excel in other "social" or "soft" skills such as leadership, communication, compassion, volunteerism, career, background, and diversity.

While this shift in mission is not a bad thing (some of the most financially successful doctors I know are academically B-average students, but with amazing bedside manners and business talent), it does come with consequences, especially when it comes to passing classes each quarter, as well as the NBEO Parts 1, 2, and 3 (which is the great equalizer).

The real tragedy in these statistics, however, is seen among international students who are not able to graduate or pass NBEO board exams. These students often attend expensive Caribbean schools that may not even qualify for federal loans (which usually have lower interest rates) with forgiveness benefits and thus are forced to take on higher-interest private loans.

In addition, a lot of the lesser-known or newer optometry schools are not experienced enough to train future optometrists or prepare them for the rigorous challenge of trying to pass boards.

So enough with the depressing reality. Here is our advice if you are in either of these situations:

If you are struggling academically, involve your academic office early on. Most optometry schools want to see their students succeed and complete the program. Extra tutoring, professor support, or additional study time to complete your studies is likely available at no additional cost. If you find yourself struggling academically, it should be a wake-up call for you to drop ALL non-essential academic activities, such as leadership organization positions, extracurricular activities, and work-study jobs and focus 100 percent on your classes.

From my experience, quite a few of my fellow classmates who struggle in the pre-clinical years do just fine on their clinical rotations during their fourth year and into residency. *They are some of the finest doctors that I know.* So If you find yourself struggling, ask for help and stay motivated. There is a lot of support out there and the school will likely find a way to get you sufficiently educated, even if it takes a little more time.

Now, let's touch on the NBEO Part 1–3 pass rate in 2021–2022:

NATIONAL BOARD OF EXAMINERS IN OPTOMETRY

October 1, 2021 – September 30, 2022 Institutional Yearly Performance Report

Schools	Number of Candidates	Part I ABS First Timer Pass Rate	Part II PAM First Timer Pass Rate	Part III CSE First Timer Pass Rate	Ultimate Pass Rate
Arizona College of Optometry at Midwestern University[1]	51	86.27%	98.04%	94.12%	98.04%
Chicago College of Optometry[3]	44	68.18%	72.73%	93.18%	95.45%
Herbert Wertheim School of Optometry & Vision Science	62	88.71%	95.16%	96.77%	98.39%
IAUPR-School of Optometry[1]	32	37.50%	40.63%	40.63%	68.75%
Illinois College of Optometry	132	81.06%	95.45%	90.15%	96.97%
Indiana University School of Optometry	69	65.22%	92.75%	78.26%	85.51%
Michigan College of Optometry[4]	36	83.33%	97.22%	77.78%	91.67%
New England College of Optometry	112	74.11%	90.18%	72.32%	89.29%
Northeastern State University, Oklahoma College of Optometry[1]	27	77.78%	96.30%	74.07%	96.30%
Nova Southeastern University College of Optometry[1]	97	72.16%	85.57%	80.41%	90.72%
Pacific University College of Optometry	87	74.71%	86.21%	85.06%	85.06%
Salus University, Pennsylvania College of Optometry	149	73.83%	81.88%	81.21%	83.89%
School of Optometry, Massachusetts College of Pharmacy & Health Sciences	51	50.98%	60.78%	68.63%	66.67%
Southern California College of Optometry at Marshall B Ketchum University	103	76.70%	86.41%	86.41%	90.29%
Southern College of Optometry[2]	120	85.00%	91.67%	79.17%	97.50%
State University of New York College of Optometry	95	87.37%	93.68%	81.05%	93.68%
The Ohio State University College of Optometry	69	92.75%	97.10%	89.86%	95.65%
University of Missouri St. Louis, College of Optometry[4]	37	86.49%	94.59%	72.97%	94.59%
University of Alabama at Birmingham, School of Optometry	39	71.79%	97.44%	74.36%	92.31%
University of Houston College of Optometry	94	73.40%	87.23%	89.36%	89.36%
University of Pikeville Kentucky College of Optometry	70	41.43%	60.00%	44.29%	60.00%
University of the Incarnate Word Rosenberg School of Optometry	50	56.00%	82.00%	76.00%	78.00%
Western University of Health Sciences	75	44.00%	70.67%	73.33%	66.67%
National	**1701**	**73.19%**	**86.01%**	**79.89%**	**87.77%**

Notes:

[1] These universities require candidates to pass Part I for graduation

[2] These universities require candidates to pass Part I and Part II for graduation

[3] These universities require candidates to attempt but not necessarily pass Part I and Part II for graduation

[4] These universities require candidates to attempt but not necessarily pass Part I, Part II, and Part III for graduation

[5] These universities require candidates to pass Part I and attempt but not necessarily pass Part II for graduation

-All pass rates are calculated using only candidates who have graduated during the listed time frame and attempted all three parts at least once.

-First Timer pass rates are the percentage of the above-referenced candidate group that passed the examination on their first attempt.

-Ultimate pass rate is the percentage of the above-referenced candidate group that passed all three exams.

-Graduation data from Canadian schools of optometry were not available at the time of the production of this report and are not included in aggregated totals.

While we acknowledge that Part 2 (clinical cases, written test) and Part 3 (clinical procedures) are superior indicators of a doctor's true knowledge and skills, *it is important to recognize that Part 1 places significant focus on one's proficiency as a test-taker and the ability to memorize extensively* (but often less so on practical information). Nevertheless, obtaining a passing grade on all three parts is a prerequisite for acquiring your doctor's license.

As evident from the NBEO statistics, the passing rates vary considerably among different schools, with some of the newer and smaller institutions having significantly below-average pass rates. **However, it is reassuring to note that the national ultimate pass rate stands at a commendable 87.77 percent.**

If you find yourself among the unfortunate students who did not pass the boards, particularly NBEO Part 1, it is essential to handle your emotions positively and reach out to your close classmates. You might discover that others are facing the same situation, which will provide solace in knowing you are not alone, and possibly a supportive study buddy for the next time around, which can make for a more enjoyable experience.

To overcome this setback, direct 100 percent of your energy and time toward preparing for the retake. I have observed that an intense six to eight weeks of review often proves more effective than spreading it over several months. A recommended program like KMK can provide a solid foundation, especially in creating personalized handwritten study guides. Try to cover all the study materials in one pass, acknowledging that remembering everything immediately is not even remotely possible or even necessary for NBEO Part 1.

For practice tests, we found that OptoPrep practice questions closely resemble those in NBEO over KMK. Make it your objective to complete a full practice test daily. Subsequently, review each question, understanding why you answered correctly or incorrectly, and refer back to your study guide as needed. **This** approach will help build stamina for the actual exam day, as Part 1 relies largely on your test-taking skills.

In times of discouragement, remembering this old joke and knowing how true this is will help you push forward: "*What do you call someone who graduates at the bottom of their optometry school class?*"

A doctor.

Stay focused on your goal, put in the extra effort to succeed academically, and keep in mind that the NBEO is the final test you will ever take for the rest of your life. So embrace the challenge and study diligently!

2. Career Change from Optometry

As an optometrist, I understand that while some individuals may have known from an early age that they wanted to pursue this career path, many of us embarked on the healthcare journey by enrolling in our first Life Science series during undergraduate studies as naive, young eighteen-year-olds or being exposed to it by our OD parents. It is quite common for nearly every professional student to experience moments of questioning their chosen career path during their education or training.

To those students who might be considering a career change or dropping out of school, I urge you to exercise caution and avoid making hasty decisions.

Take the time to reflect on what has changed since your initial enrollment as an excited first-year student. Do not let poor performance in one class or rotations compel you to drop out. Moreover, do not allow inappropriate harassment from others to push you out of the profession. If you are facing physical or mental health challenges such as depression, anxiety, substance abuse, or ADHD, I encourage you to seek help from qualified professionals and reach out to supportive peers both in person and online.

Regardless of the nature of your concerns, it is crucial to involve your dean's office early in the process. They have dealt with students in similar situations before and can offer valuable resources and suggestions that you might not have considered.

If you have determined that optometry is not the right profession for you, consider the stage of your education. If you are in the early years of your program, the burden of student debt may not be excessively high yet.

While owing $50,000–$100,000 in student loans is unfortunate, individuals who possess the intelligence and motivation to gain admission to a doctoral program have various career opportunities that can help repay those loans. Working for the optometric industry or other biotechnology companies can be viable options. However, if you find yourself in your third or fourth year of study, leaving school with several hundred thousand dollars in debt and no realistic means to repay, it becomes a more serious concern.

In such circumstances, it is essential to explore all available options. Keep in mind that having a doctor's title behind your name carries value, even if you do not pursue clinical practice.

These esteemed degrees can open doors in research, industry, and academia for individuals seeking non-clinical roles. Therefore, consider completing the degree for financial reasons, even if your current enjoyment of the program is limited.

3. Perils of Divorce, Drugs & Gambling

It may be that only a minority of your classmates are presently married; however, divorce remains a substantial potential pitfall that all prospective doctors must vigilantly bear in mind. Traditionally, optometrists have boasted one of the lowest divorce rates, *at approximately 2.9 percent, compared to the national average of 5 percent.* This is largely attributable to stable work schedules, satisfying salaries, and manageable stress levels.

However, with the escalation of student debt (averaging over $250,000) and a relatively stagnant income ($120,000–$130,000), many recent graduates are joining the workforce under significant financial pressure. These financial strains can incite conflicts in personal relationships and marriages, often resulting in delayed personal milestones such as weddings, home purchases, and family planning. This can exert additional stress on a marriage, potentially leading to divorce.

From a financial perspective, divorce typically bisects your net worth in half and can substantially impact your future income for several years, especially when taking into account child support or alimony payments. Consequently, one could argue that the most prudent financial measure for a doctor is a consistent investment in their relationship, perhaps via regular date nights.

While it may not be universally embraced, consider the benefits of a prenuptial agreement. This becomes particularly relevant if you marry after having accrued significant wealth or if there are children from a previous marriage. In some cases, a postnuptial agreement may be appropriate if both parties are amenable. Divorce laws vary state by state, with certain jurisdictions favoring men and others women. The calculations for "standard" alimony payments can vary dramatically from one state to another. As a general guideline, an optometric student or resident who divorces is unlikely to owe as much in alimony as a practicing doctor would.

Many individuals who have gone through a divorce express regret for not seeking better legal advice prior to initiating proceedings. A consistent recommendation is for both spouses to participate actively in managing the family's finances, regardless of how busy one or both parties may be due to studies or residency. Premarital counseling is also often advocated.

Interestingly, female doctors have a 50 percent higher divorce rate than their male counterparts. Although it was stated somewhat jestingly that regular date nights may be the best financial investment, in reality, it holds significant weight. A strong and supportive partner is an invaluable asset, both emotionally and mentally, for any doctor seeking genuine financial success.

Moreover, substance abuse or gambling addiction, either personally or in your partner, can lead to severe financial loss. Should such issues arise, it's imperative to seek professional help immediately. Remaining engaged with family finances will ensure that potential problems cannot be concealed for long, helping to prevent what could become the most severe form of financial infidelity.

4. Professional License Preservation: Beyond Malpractice

I won't delve extensively into the complexities of malpractice, but it's crucial to note that many doctors overlook the fact that malpractice insurance only covers a fraction of potential professional liabilities. Importantly, your malpractice policy will

NOT cover expenses incurred in the face of the following professional incidents:

- Medicare or Medicaid fraud
- Allegations of sexual harassment involving staff members
- Claims of inappropriate patient relationships
- Loss of licensure
- Revocation of hospital privileges
- Improper alteration of medical records
- Criminal activities

Each of these can trigger simultaneous lawsuits and lead to loss of income, none of which can be insured against. Therefore, it's essential to always uphold the highest standards of medical practice and conduct yourself with the utmost integrity. Cultivate a strong bedside manner with your patients, and establish good habits and routines that will shield you against false accusations. These could include diligent note-taking, abstaining from impaired driving, and maintaining professional conduct, especially toward coworkers of the opposite sex.

Remember that a doctor who is kindhearted and communicative toward their patients is less likely to be sued than a jerk-face rude doctor.

Bear in mind that due to their perceived wealth, doctors are often targeted for unfounded lawsuits. However, above all, remember that we occupy a position of trust in society.

Never jeopardize or betray this trust because in addition to risking your professional license, you could face potentially crippling financial repercussions due to lawsuits.

In summary, we sincerely hope that you will never need the information in this chapter, but if you do, just know that while it seems impossible, there is a light at the end of the tunnel with the proper mindset and hard work.

Key Takeaways:

- Academic success: Recognize the challenges in optometry programs and the need for focus and dedication in order to pass all exams. If you're struggling, reach out for help early on. Academic offices and resources are there to help students succeed.

- Career changes: Treat the decision to change careers with caution. Understand that a degree in optometry offers a range of opportunities beyond clinical practice. Consult with the dean's office or career counselor for advice and resources before making significant career decisions.

- Personal perils: Be aware of the significant financial implications of divorce, drug use, and gambling. Maintaining healthy relationships, seeking prenuptial agreements where applicable, and addressing addictions early can help avoid potential financial catastrophes.

- Professional conduct: Practice professional integrity at all times. Malpractice insurance doesn't cover all instances of professional misconduct. Uphold professional standards, conduct yourself appropriately in all interactions, and maintain diligent recordkeeping to protect against potential legal issues.

CHAPTER 7:

HOW TO PROTECT YOUR MOST VALUABLE ASSETS VIA LIFE & DISABILITY INSURANCE | BY DAT BUI, OD

Fun is like life insurance, the older you get—the more it costs.
—Kin Hubbard

In the last chapter, we discussed all the financial catastrophes that an optometrist cannot insure against, such as divorce or failing boards. But luckily certain financial catastrophes can be safeguarded against through insurance.

Financial catastrophes that you CAN insure against:

- Death of an income provider with dependents (term life insurance)
- Serious illness or injury (medical insurance)
- Disability (short- or long-term disability insurance)
- Professional liability (malpractice insurance)
- Loss of valuable personal property (rental or home-owner insurance)
- Vehicular liability (car insurance)
- Personal liability (umbrella insurance)

Since we are only focusing on optometry students in this book, we are going to focus on life and disability insurance.

(I) Term Life Insurance

Life insurance is a subject that most people shy away from, often due to its morbid nature. However, for a vast majority of individuals, especially students with dependents or anyone whose income is relied upon by others, it's crucial to consider the financial implications of their death on those left behind.

---

2 Reasons To Get Life Insurance:

1) **Income protection:** As an optometrist, there's a high likelihood that you are (or will be) your household's primary income provider, and your income is necessary for maintaining your family's living standards. Thus, it is essential to protect or, at the very least, preserve that lifestyle in the event of your death.

2) **Providing security for your family:** Knowing that your loved ones will be taken care of if anything happens to you can bring immense peace of mind.

---

2 Reasons NOT To Get Life Insurance:

1) **No dependents:** If you're single with no children and/or your elderly parents aren't reliant on your income, then life insurance might not be necessary. Ideally, the cash assets you leave behind should suffice to cover your funeral expenses, which average around $10,000.

2) **Financial independence:** If you've accumulated significant wealth such that your family could live comfortably off your investments after your death, then there's no need to incur extra costs for life insurance. However, keep in mind that unless you've received a large inheritance, this scenario is unlikely

> for most students.

Let's Discuss the Difference Between Term Life and Permanent Life Insurance:

1) **Term Life Insurance**

   This involves paying an affordable set monthly premium for a specified period in exchange for a benefit amount of your choosing. Should you die during this term, your beneficiary will receive the benefit amount tax-free.

   Example: A healthy thirty-year-old male can get a $1 million policy for a thirty-year term at $647 per year (or $53 monthly), whereas a healthy thirty-year-old female can get the same coverage at $525 per year (or $43 monthly).

2) **Whole/Permanent/Variable or Indexed Universal Life Insurance/ Infinite Banking**

   This is a more complex option. In addition to life insurance, there is an "investment" cash-value component, which significantly increases monthly premiums, almost 13x the cost of a cheaper term life policy.

   Example: A healthy thirty-year-old male can get a $1 million policy for a thirty-year term at $8,380 per year (or $698 monthly). Meanwhile, a healthy thirty-year-old female can get the same coverage for $7,417 per year (or $618 monthly).

Your beneficiaries will receive the benefit amount tax-free in the event of your death, and you can borrow against the cash value. However, withdrawing it can incur high surrender fees.

Financial Tip

Insurance and investing should NEVER be mixed. For 99 percent of the population, signing up for low-cost, straightforward TERM life insurance is the best route. Avoid whole life insurance at all costs.

Remember that whole life insurance's marketing is probably one of the most impressive when it comes to repackaging the same crappy product. Watch out for self-proclaimed social media financial "experts" selling these shady products.

How Is Your Term Life Monthly Premium Determined?

1) **Age/Sex/Health History/Smoking Status**

   Beside all these listed above, other factors can include criminal history and even driving record (such as suspensions or speeding ticket violations).

2) **Family History**

   Family history of conditions such as heart disease, diabetes, and cancer will have an impact on the cost.

3) **Coverage Amount and Term**

   The amount of the coverage (e.g., $1 million benefit) and the term (e.g., thirty years) needed will be taken into account. Obviously, the higher the amount and the longer the term, the more premium costs.

4) Risky Hobbies/Activities

If you like to skydive, rock climb, or engage in other potentially risky activities, then be prepared to have higher costs.

How Much Term Life Should I Get?

Everyone's situation is different, so the amount of life insurance needed will vary. The first step is to determine what your obligations are:

- **Future expenses:** This included things such as funeral costs, child care, elder care for your aging parents, or college tuition for your children

- **Income support:** This is the amount needed to support your family, basically what their yearly living expenses are.

- **Any significant debt remaining:** This includes things such as a home mortgage or student loan.

While these obligations might increase the total benefit needed, consider your savings and investments as well to offset those costs.

But for the majority of optometrists, a good guideline is as follows:

> ### Pre-Tax Yearly Salary x 17 = Amount of Term Life Insurance

Example: If an optometrist is the sole income provider for his/her spouse and children, with an average salary of $120,000. Then, he/she would just need to **purchase roughly $2 million worth of life insurance ($120,000 x 17)**. With this amount of coverage, the spouse should be able to replace all income with the yearly interest earned by properly investing the $2 million in a low-cost stock/bond diverse index fund.

How does this work? Assuming a conservative average yearly return of 7 percent, the yearly gain will be roughly $140,000 and can be used to support the family, without touching the original principal investment of $2 million.

Note: If your spouse can work part time after your death and your family only relies on half of your doctor's salary for their expenses, then you may only need five to ten times your salary in life insurance.

Remember that **the whole goal of life insurance is to maintain your family's comfort of living.**

How long should I get life insurance for?

Term life insurance is relatively affordable, but it's essential to ensure it doesn't exceed your monthly budget. If you miss a single payment, your life insurance could lapse, so it's crucial to make payments that fit within your budget.

The amount of term life insurance you should get should cover you until you retire or achieve financial independence, whichever comes first. Why is this? Simply because life insurance becomes more expensive as you age, owing to the increased likelihood of death and subsequent payout. (Makes sense, right?)

For example, if you're a thirty-five-year-old optometrist in excellent health earning a salary of $170,000, you could sign up for a thirty-year fixed-rate policy with $3 million coverage. This would cost roughly $2,370 a year (or about $197 a month). Should something unexpected happen to you, this policy will ensure your family is fully protected until your retirement funds become available.

Alternatively, you might choose a shorter term, like fifteen years, which would be more affordable compared to a thirty-year term. After the initial fifteen-year term expires, you could renew it for another ten or fifteen years, though be aware that you'll likely face higher premiums due to increased age-associated risk.

However, it's worth noting that many doctors might be financially secure by this point and, therefore, might not need any life insurance to support their families.

Generally speaking, we recommend a fifteen-year fixed term as the initial choice for life insurance.

What about Whole Life Insurance?

Throughout your career, you're likely to come across a variety of poor financial products, and whole life insurance ranks among them. This, in many respects, is one of the most significant financial scams that insurance salespeople use to exploit "smart" doctors.

It often masquerades under various names, including *universal, universal index, variable,* and *permanent life insurance* and now, with the advent of sketchy TikTok "financial" influencers, *infinite banking.*

Whole life insurance is marketed to provide life insurance coverage as well as a cash value policy that is supposedly invested and touted to grow tax-free. Sounds good, doesn't it? Absolutely not!

Here are three reasons why whole life insurance is a rip-off:

1) **Exorbitant fees:** Whole life insurance comes with an astoundingly high monthly premium, nearly fifteen to twenty times the cost of affordable term life insurance.

2) **Low return on investment for cash value policy:** The returns on whole life insurance are staggeringly low, averaging around 2–3 percent, but only after holding the policy for over fifteen years. Absurd, right? It's not even beating the yearly inflation rate of 3–4 percent. Many times, due to heavy upfront sales commission fees and high surrender charges (what you pay to quit the policy early), the policy yields a negative return. Often, after 10–15 years, you either break even or lose money.

3) **Unnecessary income tax or estate tax benefits:** Salespeople are quick to highlight that loans can be taken from the cash policy tax-free, claiming it's superior to your retirement or taxable account. But hold on! Shouldn't it be tax-free if you're using post-tax money to pay the premium to fund this cash policy (common sense, right?)?

Another so-called tax benefit that salespeople often promote is the death benefit of the policy, allegedly to help "wealthy" optometrists avoid estate taxes. As of 2020, estates valued at over $11.58 million per individual or $23.16 million per couple are subject to federal estate taxes—figures that most optometrists likely won't reach in their lifetime.

The essential takeaway here is to **AVOID whole life insurance at all costs**. Don't be one of those unsuspecting new grad doctors preyed on by an insurance salesperson masquerading as a financial advisor. If your financial advisor even mentions whole life insurance, give them the boot!

A more tax-efficient approach would be to purchase cheap term life insurance and invest the absurdly high whole life monthly payments in your own tax-efficient retirement accounts, such as your 401(k), Roth IRA, and other IRAs. Then funnel the remainder into a taxable brokerage account (subject to a 15–20 percent long-term capital gains tax). This strategy offers better cash liquidity and approximates the S&P 500 Stock Index average return of 10–12 percent.

Where Can I Purchase Life Insurance?

There's a host of reputable companies out there offering life insurance, but beware! There are also plenty of less-than-reputable, dubious entities peddling subpar products. In the past, it was quite a task to gather multiple quotes, but fret not! Aaron and I have done the legwork. We've vetted and researched these recommended online independent brokers who can streamline the process for you, shopping across numerous companies to find the coverage that suits your needs.

These brokers not only offer a user-friendly interface, but their team will also guide you through the entire process from application to policy signing. And guess what? You can even get an estimate without revealing your personal information!

Take a look at our **Recommended List of Insurance Agents:**

odsonfinance.com/insurance-agents.

(II) Disability Insurance: Safeguarding Your Most Precious Asset

As an optometrist, you might earn an average salary of $120,000. Over the course of your career, factoring in raises and inflation, you stand to make about $5 million. You likely invested eight to ten years in education to get here, taking out potentially more than $200,000 in student loans to secure your future. Considering the energy, time, and financial resources you've poured into your career, it becomes imperative to safeguard that doctor's income. Regardless of how meticulously you budget or engage in side hustles, your optometric profession typically generates your highest income.

Even if you're young and healthy, have you pondered your ability to support yourself and your family if an accident or illness suddenly renders you unable to work? Disability insurance offers a financial cushion to handle your bills and expenses if you're incapacitated. Hence, disability insurance essentially equates to income insurance. Long-term disability insurance shields you from income loss if an illness or injury prevents you from working for an extended period (over ninety days).

Financial Tip

Studies have revealed that 20 percent of individuals will face a period of disability before they turn sixty-five. Yet about 70 percent of private sector employees lack long-term disability insurance.

Given these statistics, it's clear that insuring against a potential financial crisis is a must.

Disability insurance is exceedingly complex and highly dependent on each person's health status, and it can vary significantly among insurers. This chapter isn't a comprehensive overview of the intricacies involved in each disability policy but is intended to serve as a basic guide, particularly for newly minted doctors.

Disability insurance pricing directly correlates to a certain percentage of your income and tends to become costlier as you age, due to the increasing likelihood of an insurance payout. Various factors can boost the amount you'll need to pay, such as engaging in a high-risk profession like stunt work or engaging in dangerous hobbies like rock climbing or skydiving. Furthermore, your general health condition plays a substantial role. Several exclusion factors exist, such as pre-existing life-threatening medical conditions that the policy won't cover.

For instance, if you had a chronic heart condition when you obtained the disability insurance and later became disabled due to a heart attack, the policy wouldn't pay out anything. (Astounding, isn't it?) There may also be limitations on payout qualifications, such as injuries incurred during foreign travel, pregnancy, or mental disorders. The list of potential limitations and exclusions goes on and on.

How Much Long-Term Disability (LTD) Insurance Should You Purchase?

Unlike life insurance, there's a strict cap on the amount of disability insurance you can buy. Generally, most insurance companies only cover up to a maximum of 66 percent of your total salary, charging an annual premium that's about 1–3 percent of your total annual income.

> We typically recommend that your LTD coverage equals **60% of your pre tax salary**.

For instance, a doctor earning an annual salary of $150,000 might pay an average annual premium of $3,000 (1–3 percent of the salary) or a monthly average payment of $250. If they become completely disabled and are unable to work, their insurance will provide roughly $90,000 a year (or 60 percent of their salary) until they reach the age of sixty-five.

Here's the average monthly cost for LTD for a healthy doctor (2023)

Age 25:	Age 30:
$125–165 per month	$130–180 per month
Age 40:	**Age 50:**
$175–240 per month	$280–375 per month

Five key factors can influence your policy rate and significantly increase the cost:

1) **Coverage amount:** The extent of coverage you need is based on your current income and the amount necessary to maintain your desired lifestyle. The higher the

coverage, the more expensive your insurance rate. A good rule of thumb is to aim for coverage equal to 60 percent of your pre-tax gross salary.

2) **Benefit period:** This is the duration over which you want the benefits to last. It can range from a few years to a decade or even until retirement. The longer the benefit period, the more expensive it'll be. We recommend a minimum of at least five years, but if you can afford more, go for it!

3) **Waiting period:** This is the time lapse between when you become disabled and when you start receiving disability benefits. A shorter waiting period makes the policy costlier. To bridge this waiting period, many doctors maintain an emergency fund (three to six months) to cover their expenses or opt for short-term disability insurance (discussed later). We advise maintaining a substantial emergency fund to help mitigate the cost of a shorter waiting period.

4) **Age and health:** Older or less healthy individuals will find disability insurance to be more expensive. Hence, when purchasing disability insurance, it's never going to be cheaper than it is today.

5) **Occupation:** Riskier professions (for example, being a stuntman) lead to higher insurance costs. Fortunately, optometry is considered a relatively low-risk profession. After all, refracting isn't exactly life-threatening.

These five crucial factors establish the base price for typical LTD coverage for a few years, resulting in premiums that cost only about 1 percent of your annual salary. However, if you want more comprehensive protection with a longer benefit period, your premiums could amount to nearly 3 percent of your annual salary.

Additional features, referred to as *riders*, can be added to your policy, but these will incur extra fees.

What Are Five Features/Riders an Optometrist Might Need?

1) **Non-cancellable option:** This ensures your insurance company can't cancel your policy or hike your premium rate if you switch jobs to pursue a passion like professional skydiving.

2) **Own-occupation policy:** This enables you to continue receiving disability benefits if you're too disabled to resume your work as an optometrist, even if you can undertake other types of work, such as becoming an internet blogger. It's different from an "any occupation" policy, which only pays benefits if you're too disabled to perform any kind of work. THIS IS THE MOST IMPORTANT.

3) **Student loan rider:** This rider allows you to secure additional coverage to pay off student loan balances while disabled. It's particularly crucial for those who might refinance with a private lender and consequently won't be able to benefit from federal loan forgiveness in the event of disability.

4) **Future purchase option:** This provision allows you to enhance your coverage in the future without needing to provide additional proof of medical insurability. It's a great choice for young doctors who anticipate their income will grow over time.

5) **Partial or residual disability benefits:** This rider pays a benefit even if you're still able to work part-time as an

optometrist but experience a substantial loss of income (due to fewer working hours or reduced productivity) resulting from an injury.

There are many other types of riders that various insurance companies offer. While these options are great and can be tailored to your specific personal situation, it's evident that not all types of riders are necessary. It's vital to consult with a disability insurance agent/broker to ensure you have all the protection you require.

Financial Tip

Remember that the most important rider to get for your long-term disability policy is an **own-occupation policy**. This enables you to continue receiving disability benefits if you're too disabled to resume your work as an optometrist, even if you can undertake other types of work, such as becoming an internet blogger. It's different from an "any occupation" policy, which only pays benefits if you're too disabled to perform any kind of work.

What about Short-term Disability Insurance (STD)?

Short-term disability insurance (STD) effectively substitutes your income for a short duration (typically three to six months). STD can cover that waiting period before your long-term disability insurance activates. Some female doctors might opt for a short-term disability policy specifically tailored to cover future planned pregnancies. *However, for the majority of us, maintaining a substantial emergency fund of around six months should be sufficient to bridge any brief period of income loss.*

When Should You Consider Buying Disability Insurance?

Did you know that as an optometry student, you can actually purchase disability insurance? In fact, some schools even offer it as part of their package. However, from my own personal perspective, the best time to take this step is when you begin your professional journey and start earning—be it as a resident or a practicing doctor.

Here's something else to keep in mind: *disability insurance probably won't ever be as affordable for you as it is today.* That's just the way it works—the price generally increases as we age and as our health changes. The costs can vary too. For example, your location can impact the cost (California isn't exactly the most affordable state for insurance) and so can your gender (insurance companies tend to charge women more, so it might be a good idea to seek out a gender-neutral policy). Your health condition and even your hobbies can affect the pricing, though they're typically excluded from the policy rather than factored into the cost.

In summary, remember that there are lots of ways to lose your ability to practice optometry, and your largest asset is your potential to earn a doctor's income. Death and disability insurance are two great ways to protect yourself and your family in the event of death or disability.

Key Takeaways:

- Cheap term life insurance provides income protection and peace of mind for anyone who relies on your income as a doctor. However, it's unnecessary for those without dependents or with significant wealth. Usually an $1 million policy is recommended for a typical doctor. A guideline for optometrists: pre-tax yearly salary x 17.

- Beware of whole life insurance! It has high fees and low returns and isn't usually necessary. Instead, invest the monthly premium in other tax-efficient accounts.

- Despite 20 percent of people likely facing a disability before age sixty-five, around 70 percent of private sector workers don't have long-term disability insurance, underscoring its importance.

- Typically, long-term disability (LTD) insurance covers up to 66 percent of a doctor's salary. Recommended coverage is 60 percent of one's pre tax salary, with premiums ranging between 1 and 3 percent of annual income.

- Several additional features, or riders, can customize a policy, including non-cancellable options, own-occupation policies, student loan riders, future purchase options, and partial/residual disability benefits. But the most important rider to add on is the own-occupation rider!

- Short-term disability insurance (STD) covers income for short durations (three to six months), acting as a bridge before LTD kicks in. An emergency fund of around six months can also serve this purpose.

CHAPTER 8:

PREVENTING BURNOUT AS AN OPTOMETRY STUDENT | BY CHRIS LOPEZ, OD

Burnout is the result of too much energy output and not enough energy self-invested.

—Melissa Steginus

Burnout is real, and optometry school is not easy. Juggling classes, clinical rotations, studying, and personal responsibilities can take a toll on one's mental and physical health, leading to a decrease in productivity, motivation, and overall well-being.

Couple this with the student loan burden that so many optometry students face, and it's no wonder why so many ODs feel fatigued. (Don't worry, reading this book will have you well on your way to paying off student loan debt!) On the bright side, being an optometry student is also an exciting and rewarding experience. Below are some strategies to help you combat burnout and make the most of your time during optometry school.

Exercise

Of all the strategies on this list, exercise is the tool that helped me the most during my time in optometry school (and even now as a practicing OD). There is a breadth of research demonstrating the positive impact exercise may have on overall well-being, but I won't bore readers with talk of endorphins.

The neat thing is that there is not one particular type of training that is necessary. With that in mind, there is bound to be a workout that appeals to each individual—weightlifting, CrossFit, yoga, running, boxing, swimming, and more.

Carving out time to exercise and making it a PRIORITY is the only way to ensure that it is done on a consistent basis. No, it's not easy to wake up at 6:00 a.m. and work out before class. No, you don't always have time during lunch break to head to the gym. Yes, it does suck to squeeze in a late-night training session after eating dinner and studying. However, exercising can keep your mind sharp and your body healthy during stressful times. Not to mention, no one has ever completed a workout and regretted it.

Financial Tip

Exercise falls under the umbrella of self-care. Also prioritize getting enough sleep and eating healthy. When self-care is prioritized, more energy and focus is present to dedicate toward becoming the best doctor possible.

Set Realistic Goals

One of the main reasons students experience burnout is that they set unrealistic goals for themselves. It's important to set objectives that are challenging but achievable. This means breaking down large goals into smaller, more manageable tasks and creating a plan to accomplish them. This approach can help you avoid feeling overwhelmed and help you stay motivated throughout your studies.

It also helps to build a sense of accomplishment and motivation to continue.

Time Management

Effective time management is critical for preventing burnout as an optometry student. This means creating a schedule that allows you to balance your academic responsibilities with your personal life. Use a planner or calendar to map out your assignments, exams, and other commitments to help maximize scholarly and personal achievement in a timely manner.

Stay Organized

With a heavy course load, lab work, clinical rotations, and studying for exams, it can be challenging to have everything sorted appropriately. Staying organized is essential for success during optometry school. Keep track of important deadlines and assignments with a planner/calendar. Create a study schedule that allows for regular breaks and time to review material. Use digital tools like note-taking apps to stay organized and keep track of important information. Finally, keep a tidy study area to help reduce distractions and improve focus, which can lead to better productivity and success.

Seek Support

Students have many challenges to navigate during their time in academia. Fortunately, there are a variety of resources, including tutoring and study groups, counseling services, and peer support groups, that can help to maintain overall well-being.

Optometry students may also seek support from their professors, clinical supervisors, or professional organizations. It is important to recognize and pursue assistance *before* challenges become overwhelming. Doing so allows for increased motivation, the development of coping skills, and the building of a strong support system, which are beneficial throughout the academic and professional journey.

Practice Mindfulness

Practicing mindfulness involves being fully present in the moment and paying attention to one's thoughts and feelings. In doing so, students can develop a greater awareness of their mental and emotional state, which can help with managing stress and anxiety more effectively. Some mindfulness practices to incorporate into a daily routine include breathing exercises, meditation, or simply taking a few minutes each day to focus on thoughts and emotions. Meditation is not witchcraft, and it's not hocus pocus. In fact, countless well-conducted scientific studies have demonstrated the efficacy of meditation and mindfulness practices in promoting happiness, increasing efficiency, and reducing stress. Improving focus and concentration and promoting a sense of calm and balance in your life can go a long way in making optometry school a more enjoyable experience.

Get Sleep

It may seem that the terms *adequate sleep* and *doctorate program* are seemingly at odds with each other, but the importance of getting sleep during optometry school cannot be overstated.

Many studies have shown that sleep contributes to both memory and cognitive function—so pulling all-nighters may not be the wisest thing for your grades or your future as a clinician. Also keep in mind that decreased sleep is directly correlated with a myriad of cardiovascular and neurological issues—so even though you've got a massive workload, try to aim for at least six to eight hours of sleep per night (easier said than done, I know!).

Big Picture

Lastly, always try to keep the big picture in mind. At the end of a few challenging years, we all become DOCTORS—an accomplishment that many of us have yearned for since childhood. We will all have the tools to be successful. We can all become outstanding clinicians and provide top-notch care to our patients. With the help of this book, you can crush your student loan debt and start your career off on the right foot. Most importantly, we can use our skills and influence to do good in this world.

Optometry school is no joke. It takes a lot of work, time, and determination to achieve good grades, develop technical and practical skills, and transform into a well-rounded clinician. Utilize the strategies above to manage stress and amplify overall well-being. Do the most to ensure a successful and fulfilling career in optometry. Our ODs On Finance team believes in you!

Key Takeaways:

- Burnout in optometry school: The combination of rigorous academics, personal responsibilities, and student loan burdens can lead to significant mental and physical strain.

- Importance of self-care: Prioritizing exercise, adequate sleep, and healthy eating can significantly improve well-being and academic performance.

- Effective study habits: Setting realistic goals, managing time efficiently, and staying organized are essential for success and prevent being overwhelmed.

- Support and mindfulness: Seeking academic and emotional support, along with practicing mindfulness, can help manage stress and maintain a balanced perspective during challenging times. Remember the light at the end of the tunnel.

PART II

SET YOURSELF UP FOR SUCCESS WHILE IN SCHOOL

CHAPTER 9:

THE ECONOMICS OF RESIDENCY — TO BE OR NOT TO | BY CHRIS LOPEZ, OD

If a man knows not to which port he sails, no wind is favorable.
—Seneca the Younger

After graduating from optometry school, the next step for many optometrists is deciding whether or not to pursue a residency. An optometry residency is a post-graduate training program that provides additional clinical experience and specialized training in a specific area of optometry. The decision to pursue a residency can be difficult, and it requires careful consideration of several ideas.

Career Goals

One of the most critical factors to consider when deciding whether to pursue a residency is your career goals. If your objective is to specialize in a particular area of optometry, then a residency may be the right choice for you. Likewise, residencies tend to be preferred by employers for certain practice settings, such as academia and VA hospitals. One of the neat things about optometry is just how many residency/specialty options there are to choose from, including low vision/vision rehabilitation, vision therapy/binocular vision, specialty contact lenses, ocular disease, and more.

Financial Tip

Please keep in mind that much of the dialogue being used in support of pursuing a residency is outdated. Plenty of employers are doing away with residency requirements.

Time and Commitment

Optometry residencies are generally one-year programs that require a significant time commitment. Residents often work long hours, which can limit time for personal pursuits. It is essential to consider whether you are willing and able to commit the time required for a residency. On the other hand, many residents feel that the one-year grind was completely worth it for the knowledge and experience gained.

Financial Considerations

Residency programs can be a source of financial struggle, as residents do not receive nearly the same level of compensation as non-resident practicing ODs. **There is no set resident annual salary, but it can range from around $33,000 up to about $65,000.**

Compare this to associate optometrists in saturated markets making $110,000 annually and rural associates taking home upward of $200,000. It is essential to consider the financial impact of a residency, including the opportunity cost for the resident year, living expenses, and student loan payments—not to mention building an emergency fund or saving for retirement.

The opportunity cost is so high, given a surplus of high-paying optometry jobs available coupled with the increasing cost of tuition, that the majority of fourth-year optometry students are forgoing pursuing a residency. In fact, many have stated that the number of residency applicants has been in decline. Looking at the numbers, it's tough to blame them!

Quite a few residents moonlight in their (limited) spare time to earn extra funds. Be sure to check with your residency supervisor and site to see if it's allowed in your position.

Additionally, pursuing a residency can delay loan repayment, and interest can accrue on the loans, which can increase the total amount owed.

Financial Tip

As a contract consultant, I want you all to be aware that throughout the many hundreds of contract reviews that I have performed and the one thousand-plus ODs that I have spoken with over the past few years, the vast majority of optometrists do NOT receive higher compensation after completing a residency.

Competition

Optometry residency programs can be highly competitive, and the application process can be challenging. You will need to have a strong academic record, impressive interview abilities, and excellent communication and interpersonal skills to be considered for a residency program.

It's worth weighing potential options in the scenario that you do not match for your desired residency spot. In other words, think about a backup plan in case residency doesn't pan out.

From an employer standpoint, some private practice employers *may* prefer candidates who have completed a residency, as it can demonstrate a commitment to excellence and a willingness to pursue advanced training. However, the majority of employers do not actively seek to hire residency-trained optometrists.

Professional Networking

One of the biggest benefits of a residency experience is the opportunity to build a solid network of colleagues. During a residency, optometrists have the opportunity to work with and learn from experts in their field. Developing a network of friends and mentors who can provide guidance and support throughout a career is priceless.

Moreover, quite a few consulting, publishing, and lecturing opportunities are offered to well-connected residents that may be harder to come by for non-resident ODs. In short, residencies can open doors that may not have been available to ODs without the residency experience.

Personal Growth

A residency can be a great opportunity for personal growth and professional development. Residents gain valuable experience and increase their confidence working with patients, developing new skills, and creating relationships with mentors and colleagues.

It is crucial to consider whether a residency aligns with your personal and professional goals and whether it will help you grow and develop as an optometrist.

I often tell optometry students that personal growth is the MAIN reason to pursue a residency, in my opinion. If you do it for the money, you will likely be disappointed because a residency can provide valuable training and experience but usually does NOT lead to a higher salary (contrary to popular belief). If you do it for the opportunity for optometric fame, you should cool your ego, as there are only a select few optometrists who make a living from consulting, publishing, and lecturing.

Final Thoughts

Although an optometry residency can provide valuable training and experiences, it is not necessary for career success. Careful consideration should be taken to weigh the importance of career objectives, financial implications, and personal goals before deciding whether to pursue a residency. In short, follow the residency route for the *right* reasons. You can be successful either way!

Key Takeaways:

- Career goals and choices: residencies offer specialized training in various optometry areas, but many employers no longer require them.

- Financial implications: residencies often come with lower salaries compared to practicing ODs, and pursuing one can delay loan repayments and accrue more interest.

- Competition and networking: while residencies can be competitive, they offer invaluable networking opportunities, opening doors to unique professional experiences.

- Personal growth vs. monetary gain: residencies can significantly contribute to personal and professional growth, but they don't necessarily lead to higher salaries. Pursue them for growth, not financial benefits.

CHAPTER 10:

THE ECONOMICS OF MODALITIES, REGIONS & GENDER | BY AARON NEUFELD, OD

*If you don't value your time, neither will others.
Stop giving away your time and talents. Value
what you know and start charging for it.*
—Kim Garst

One of the greatest aspects of being an optometrist is the sheer number of directions you can take in your career path. While many optometrists choose the "standard" route of seeing patients day in and day out, other optometrists may choose careers working in academia or conducting research. Alongside this, some optometrists may choose to go their whole careers as employees, while others might catch the ownership bug very early on and never look back.

Let's take a look at a few of the most common modalities of practicing optometry, the duties entailed in that modality, and the average income that the modality produces. Income levels cited in the next few paragraphs were taken from 2022 surveys conducted by the American Optometric Association and *Review of Optometry* publication.

(I) The Economics of Modalities

When we think about the modalities of optometry, eight specific types represent the majority of optometrist positions:

1. Private practice—associate
2. Private practice—owner
3. Corporate
4. Hospital/VA
5. OD/MD
6. Academia
7. Military
8. Industry/research

1. Private Practice—Associate

> - Average annual income: $131,565
>
> - Method of compensation: per diem/salary/percentage of gross production

Being an employed optometrist at a private practice puts you in a decisive situation. You are likely to be compensated fairly, and flexibility for negotiating your compensation seems to be at its max with private practice. Due to the lack of a corporate structure or a flock of ophthalmologists hovering over your head, you tend to have more leeway in your style of practice and your scope. Production bonuses are also commonplace in private practice, and if you're good, these can be very lucrative.

One of the biggest benefits of working in a private practice is the future possibility of purchasing the practice or becoming a partner.

This possibility, if available, is something that should be clearly defined between you and the owner(s) of the practice BEFORE or AT THE START of your employment. If you are, in fact, working in a practice with the possibility of later ownership, you have two jobs: (1) be a fantastic optometrist and serve your patients well, and (2) constantly watch and take notes on every nook and cranny of the office.

So what are the cons of employed private practice work? It is possible to get lowballed for your compensation, especially if you are a new graduate or are in an oversaturated area.

Financial Tip

For example, co-author Dat recounts his personal experience as a new & naive 2015 graduate working in the Bay Area, CA. He naively agreed to a skewed production bonus that heavily favored the private practice owner, leading him to earn only $125 daily for two weeks. Shocking, isn't it?

Beware of shady practice owners who will take advantage of new graduates!

Additionally, if you have plans to take over the practice, but the owner thinks differently or you uncover some secrets you wish you did not see, your career can essentially stagnate, which probably will result in you looking for new employment.

2. Private Practice—Owner

- Average annual income: $192,409 (solo) to $285,183 (partnership/group)

- Method of compensation: salary + distributions

With great risk comes great reward—and being a practice owner perfectly illustrates that mantra. Being a private practice owner is often represented as the pinnacle or gold standard of being a successful optometrist. It statistically places you in the slot of high earner and generally garners a fair amount of respect. But like everything that is too good to be true, there is a catch.

Practice ownership has the potential to make you very rich or very poor. The deciding factor is a hodge-podge of variables, including your skill as a practitioner, your savviness as a business owner, your drivenness as a proponent/marketer, and plain luck. Starting cold can be especially daunting. There may be a period of years where you do not produce a profit. And just like any other business, there is always the possibility of failure.

When you get past all the obstacles that make your stomach churn and keep you awake at night, you find that there are some luxuries to be had as a practice owner. You can make your own hours and pay yourself what you deem appropriate. Remember when we talked about a business needing to make money off of you as an employee and thus consistently undervalue you monetarily? That need not apply to a practice owner.

3. Corporate—Sublease/Associate

- Average annual income: $153,529

- Method of compensation: salary + distributions (sublease), per diem/salary/production based (assoc.)

Corporate optometry refers to optometry practiced in offices owned by large corporations, often referred to as *chain stores*. Large corporations generally own the optical section of the office and maintain control of glasses and contact lens sales. These corporations either sublease space to optometrists or employee optometrists based on state law. Subleasing involves renting a space in the corporation's store to an optometrist and taking either rent or a portion of exam fees (or both). Employment involves either a salary or hourly pay scale for performing exams.

Ease of sliding into productive practice probably best describes the corporate modality. Employment is relatively available, even in saturated cities. **The icing on the cake is you normally get a pretty good starting rate.** Taking a sublease in a high-volume corporate office nearly guarantees a solid payday.

So what are the drawbacks? Well, first of all, there is immense pressure to sell products. After all, the corporation is enlisting your services to help produce sales. This is part of the reason your starting salary will probably be pretty decent. However, you will soon learn that your pay really is not going to increase much. Why? Because the corporation does not have an economic need to do this. If you decide to quit because of stagnating pay, they simply hire another optometrist. Unlike private practice, corporations generally rely on their brand image and promotions to keep their patient base, rather than the familiarity of doctors.

Then there is the stigma of working corporate. Many private practitioners and academics view the corporate model as *a lesser form of optometry due to restrictions placed on the practice scope by the corporation and the overarching pressure to be a salesman.* But is corporate optometry really the bastard child that relishes in conveyor belt refractions? Not necessarily. Practicing to your full scope and allowing your patients to experience exemplary care are within your reach. If you find yourself settling into a corporate optometry career, leverage your strengths and skills not only to benefit your patients, but also to make you a happier practitioner.

4. Hospital/VA

- Average annual income: $144,014

- Method of compensation: salary

Working as an optometrist in a hospital or VA setting allows for a high exposure to medical optometry in a fast-paced environment. Salary surveys point to these settings as averaging slightly below corporate and private practice. While growth may be slower in this setting, long-term commitment coupled with quality work may result in promotions to more lucrative positions such as director.

Additionally, being in a primarily medical setting allows an optometrist access to a network of expansion. Opportunities to be involved in research and lecture on the side (whether it be academia or pharma) are far more likely to pop up for someone inundated in medical cases, allowing for another stream of revenue.

5. OD/MD

- Average annual income: $131,492

- Method of compensation: salary or production based

Much like the hospital/VA setting, optometrists in the OD/MD setting find themselves surrounded by high level medical eyecare in a fast paced, high volume setting. The main difference between the hospital/VA setting and the OD/MD settings is that of being a private practice vs. a large organization. This can have pros and cons. On the pros side, there may be additional leeway with how you practice and/or negotiate your pay, in addition to not having to work weekends. On the cons side, there is less regulation than in a large hospital setting—which can sometimes lead to ODs being overworked.

6. Academia

- Average annual income: $159,778

- Method of compensation: salary

Before we even begin to discuss the financial pros and cons of practicing optometry in the academic setting, *it is important to note that most individuals entering academia do not have financials at the top of their priority list.* And rightfully so, professors and researchers enter their fields because they love what they do. They make new clinical discoveries and they enrich the minds of future practitioners.

That being said, if you do plan to enter Academia and have financial goals, it is important to know the facts. Amongst all the salary survey studies, *Academia consistently ranks as one that does not have much growth potential when it comes to salary.* This makes sense considering the economics of running a not-for-profit institution of higher education. Although tuition rates may be high, the school is always incurring losses, most notably in its clinics, where future doctors learn their trade by making mistakes over and over again. Although pay may be lower, benefits offered by academic institutions tend to be fairly good.

7. Military

- Average annual income: $131,000

- Method of compensation: salary (most fall under GS-14 or GS-15 pay scale)

We briefly touch on this in *Chapter 3: How To Pay for School* where we highlight the pros and cons of the scholarship in greater detail. But entering into a military scholarship program presents an interesting conundrum for an optometrist. The idea behind a military scholarship is simple: you get your schooling paid for in exchange for providing your (eventual) doctor skills to the military for a set time period.

The positives with this modality are that you enter the workforce debt-free and have the honor of serving your country with your optometric skills. The negatives reflect in lifestyle and pay scale. There is a chance the military may place you in an area that you do not necessarily wish to live in.

Additionally, the compensation for your "service time," normally 3 years, is quite a bit below the national average. This begs the question that if you took an "above average" job straight out of school, could you pay off your loans in that three year time span and end up with some extra cash?

8. Industry/Research

> - Average annual income: $120,000 (entry-level)— $200,000 (managerial)
>
> - Method of compensation: salary or salary + production

The industry/research position is by far the most open-ended position an optometrist can land. It can span anywhere from conducting clinical trials to traveling the nation marketing the newest daily soft contact lens to fellow doctors. Salary can vary greatly in the industry, depending on if an optometrist is taking on a leadership role vs. a more "boots on the ground" role. One thing is for certain in industry/research—the OD will most likely not be involved in traditional patient care.

(II) The Economics of Regions

When looking at total optometrist compensation, the old real estate adage has ranged true for many years: "Location, location, location."

Salary surveys often break up the US into five regions, which we have listed below from highest average salary (1) to lowest average salary (5):

1. The Midwest
2. The Northeast
3. The South
4. The Mid-Atlantic/Lower Great Lakes
5. The West

Many factors come into play when looking at regionality and associated compensation:

1) **Saturation**—Areas that are desirable to live in by definition tend to have more individuals living there, including optometrists. Couple this with optometry school locations (which often manage to feed more out of town ODs into the locality); and you have a recipe for producing too many optometrists for a given area.

   Potential patients are given the option of choice in practitioners, which in turn, based on the laws of economics dictates lower prices in order to remain competitive. The lower prices and fewer patients ultimately trickle down to the compensation of the provider. Saturation issues are especially prevalent in populous parts of California and New York, as well as other large cities.

2) **Demand**—The antithesis to saturation, demand pops up in areas that are under served. Most often this occurs in rural or semi-rural areas, but may also occur in more specialized circumstances: such as a new suburban community brought on by a burgeoning industry, or a high cost area that may have rent prices that are cost prohibitive.

3) **Cost of Living**—While cost of living does not directly affect compensation, it provides a barometer for cost of goods, staff wages and real estate prices (whether leasing or owning) of a practice in a given area. More than likely, areas with high costs of living will have higher costs in all three of these categories. These costs ultimately get passed down to the doctor in the form of lower wages.

4) **Prevalence of Vision Plans**—Despite the marketing that various vision plans do toward students, it's important to understand how they work at a fundamental business level. Vision plans are offered to various individuals, most often through workplace health insurance plans. The individuals holding these plans either pay a monthly rate for them or have their workplace do so. The vision plan will then give the individual a list of practices to choose from that accept their vision plan. The practices that accept the vision plan sign a contract in which they agree to the vision plan rules, reimbursement for services (much lower than what is considered industry average), and, in some cases, assignment of an optical laboratory mandated by the vision plan.

Thus, the vision plan operates as a gatekeeper to both new and existing patients while also double dipping in nearly all aspects of revenue that takes place during a patient encounter. So in areas where there is a prevalence of vision plans, a practice will be making far less per patient than if they were collecting through a standard cash-pay route.

In addition to the four reasons listed above, **logistics surrounding these four reasons factor into overall compensation**.

Perhaps a great practice that has its systems all figured out with handsome compensation to its associate ODs decides it wants to expand but is met with state laws that prohibit another office from opening, or there is no building or land availability for a new practice, or a vision plan that is dominant in the area prevents the second location from joining the panel—all of these realities could play into the web of reasons for why regional compensation is what it is.

(III) The Economics of Gender

It's no secret that a disparity exists between male and female earnings in optometry. The disparity varies per year, but also tilts at least moderately in favor of male optometrists. (Please keep in mind that all gender salary polls available at the time of publishing this book only split between male and female).

While the reasoning for the so-called gender gap in wages has yet to be definitively stated, in reality it is probably from a combination of factors. If we remove the factor of maternal leave from the equation, two prevailing themes emerge, which we believe, when addressed, can bring the wage delta closer for both sides.

1. **Females are less likely to negotiate than men (a general trend noted in a Harvard study).**
2. **Females are less likely to pursue practice ownership than men.**

With the trend of more and more female optometrists graduating from optometry school, it is even more important that negotiation happens to ensure fair and appropriate compensation.

Financial Tip

Female students: remember your worth, don't be afraid to seek help with negotiating your salary, and when the time is right, pull the trigger on owning your own practice.

A 2019 article from the AOA was aptly titled "The Future Is Female." While the total population of optometrists still skews in favor of males, more females are graduating from optometry school every year. We are excited to see how our profession continues to evolve through time and how the gender shift will play a role!

Key Takeaways:

- Each modality of practice will have a different level of income, so ensure that you know what that level of income is for your preferred mode of practice and plan your finances accordingly.

- Where you practice matters number-wise. Denser populations often mean more competition and less income, while the cost of living is higher. When selecting a geographic location to start your career, consider geographic trends and how they relate to income.

- Gender income disparities still exist; however, the new generation of ODs is bucking the trend, and you are a part of that revolution!

CHAPTER 11:

CAREER PREPPING DURING OPTOMETRY SCHOOL | BY CHRIS LOPEZ OD

Failing to plan is planning to fail.
—Benjamin Franklin

Career Prepping During Optometry School

Navigating the intricate maze of professional schooling is a formidable challenge. Optometry school demands academic excellence and the foresight to prepare for a successful career **beyond** the classroom. Academic knowledge, though essential, is just one facet of the multifaceted gem that is career preparation. As you, as an aspiring optometrist, transition from a first-year to a fourth-year student to a practicing OD, it becomes imperative to equip yourself with a myriad of skills, insights, and experiences that set the foundation for your future career. This chapter delves into the importance of holistic career preparation during **each** year of optometry school and the strategies you can employ as a student to ensure not only clinical proficiency but also career success. In short, follow this blueprint to make the most of your educational journey and create the foundation to cultivate personal and professional prosperity.

Year 1

The first year of optometry education is an interesting time. Excitement abounds, as well as nervousness, pride, and even a sense of intimidation. Year one provides an opportunity to establish effective habits that set the stage for a successful optometry school tenure.

Here are some key steps you can take to ensure a smooth transition and a successful first year:

Review Key Prerequisite Knowledge

Optometry school builds upon the foundational knowledge gained during your undergraduate studies. Year one material is heavily based on classes that you should already be familiar with given the prerequisite requirements of the application process. Take some time to refresh your understanding of subjects like biology, chemistry, and physics. Doing so will help you feel more confident and prepared when you start your optometry courses. Additionally, familiarizing yourself with the curriculum will help you identify any areas where you might need additional preparation.

Attend Orientation and Pre-School Events

Most optometry schools organize orientation programs and events to help incoming students get acclimated to the campus and the curriculum. Attend these events to learn more about the school's expectations, resources, and support services. It's also an excellent opportunity to meet your fellow classmates and start building a network. This is usually how initial optometry friendships are created!

Develop Good Study Habits

Optometry school requires a significant amount of studying and self-discipline. Start cultivating good study habits *before* you begin your first year. Create a study schedule that allows for dedicated time to review material, complete assignments, and prepare for exams.

Get a feel for which study techniques work best for you—active learning, breaking down complex topics into manageable parts, reading textbooks, using flashcards, etc.

The MOST important item is simply to study *consistently.* Too many first-year students think they will breeze through their courses due to subject familiarity and the idea that courses are in large part a review of undergraduate material. However, taking even one week off can lead to an overwhelming amount of class material to make up, and it only takes one poor test score to tank a semester grade. Good habits are key to success!

Stay Organized

Optometry school can be demanding, and staying organized is crucial to managing your time and responsibilities effectively. Invest in a planner or digital calendar to keep track of important dates, assignments, and study sessions. Create a system for organizing notes, lecture slides, and study materials, whether it's using physical folders or digital files.

Over half of the students in my class downloaded lecture slides on their tablet devices and used software from an inexpensive app to take notes. Being organized will help you stay on top of your coursework and reduce stress.

Seek Additional Resources

Optometry school can be challenging, but remember that there are numerous resources available to support your learning. Familiarize yourself with the school's library, research databases, and online resources. Explore opportunities for tutoring, study groups, and faculty office hours.

Take advantage of any academic support services or workshops offered by the school to enhance your learning experience.

Maintain a Healthy Work-Life Balance

While it's essential to dedicate time and effort to your studies, it's equally important to maintain a healthy work-life balance. Engage in activities that help you relax, unwind, and recharge. Prioritize physical exercise, hobbies, healthy eating, and social connections to keep your overall well-being in check. Remember that burnout can hinder your academic performance, so taking care of your physical and mental self is crucial.

Begin Building Your Professional Network

The first year of optometry school is when you're likely to have the most free time. Take advantage of the *easiest* year of optometry school by developing your online professional network, mainly LinkedIn. Creating a profile is a no-brainer for doctors and those in the eye care industry. LinkedIn is already one of the more influential professional platforms for working-class professionals, and many optometrists utilize it frequently for networking and consulting opportunities.

Stay Motivated and Engaged

Optometry school is a long journey, so it's essential to stay motivated and engaged throughout your first year. Remind yourself of the reasons why you chose this path and visualize your future career goals. Actively participate in class discussions, ask questions, and seek opportunities for hands-on experiences.

Engaging with the material and staying curious will make the learning process more enjoyable and rewarding. Keep the end game in mind—you will soon be a doctor and start your journey toward helping patients and earning a comfortable wage!

Preparing for optometry school requires commitment, dedication, and a proactive approach. By following these tips and staying focused, you'll be well-prepared to excel in your first year and set a solid foundation for the rest of your optometry education.

Year 2

Congratulations on completing your first year of optometry school! As you move into the second year, you'll be building upon the knowledge and skills you acquired during year one. Here are some strategies to help you tackle the challenges of the year two:

Review First-Year Material

Optometry school curriculum often builds upon concepts learned in the previous year. Take some time to review key topics and refresh your understanding of first-year material. This will help reinforce your knowledge and ensure a smooth transition into more advanced coursework.

Adjust Your Study Techniques

As you progress in optometry school, the complexity of the material and the workload increases. Evaluate your study techniques and adapt them accordingly.

Experiment with different approaches, such as creating concept maps, using mnemonic devices, or teaching the material to a study partner. Find what works best for you and refine your study methods.

Embrace Clinical Skills Training

Second year is when most optometry schools introduce clinical skills training. Embrace this hands-on experience and make the most of it. Practice techniques such as refraction, ophthalmoscopy, and slit lamp examination. Seek feedback from professors and clinical supervisors to enhance your skills. Actively engage in patient encounters and case discussions to develop your clinical reasoning abilities. PRACTICE, PRACTICE, PRACTICE!

Get Involved

After one full year of optometric education, most students have a sense of the workload and balancing their studies with non-school interests. Now that a more comfortable flow has been established, use this time to begin your involvement with extracurricular activities on campus. Join the private practice club or another group through your optometry institution. If you have a special interest that isn't being addressed by current organizations (like finance), then consider starting your own! Our ODs on Finance team would be happy to help you overcome the hurdles required to create your own club on campus if you reach out to us.

Develop Time-Management Skills

The workload in the second year of optometry school can be demanding. Strengthen your time-management skills to balance your coursework, clinical responsibilities, and personal commitments. Prioritize tasks, create a realistic schedule, and break down larger projects into manageable steps. Regularly review your progress and make adjustments as needed to stay organized and focused.

Seek Mentors and Networking Opportunities

Cultivate relationships with faculty members, clinicians, and practicing optometrists who can serve as mentors. They can provide guidance, share their experiences, and offer valuable insights into the profession. Take advantage of networking events, guest lectures, and professional organizations to meet new people and learn from experts in the field. Second year is a wonderful time to begin going to optometry conferences and building your network.

Maintain a Healthy Work-Life Balance

Just as in your first year, it's crucial to prioritize self-care and maintain a healthy work-life balance. Dedicate time for physical exercise, relaxation, and hobbies. Maintain connection with friends and family. Remember that taking care of yourself is essential for your overall success and happiness.

Tackling the second year of optometry education requires building upon your foundation, refining study techniques, and embracing experiences. Stay dedicated and seek support when needed.

By this point you should be well-equipped to excel in school and continue your journey toward becoming a skilled optometrist.

Year 3

Year two is complete. Now it's time to crush year three! The third year of optometry school is an exciting time to greatly expand clinical knowledge and begin making the most of patient encounters in the clinic. Use the tips below to conquer the third year of your optometric education:

Reflect on Previous Years

Take some time to reflect on your experiences in the first and second years of optometry school. Identify your strengths, your areas for improvement, and the topics that you found particularly interesting. Use this self-reflection to guide your focus and goals for the third year.

Enhance Clinical Skills

By the third year, you should have a solid foundation in clinical skills. However, there is always room for improvement. Actively seek feedback from clinical supervisors and faculty to refine your techniques. Most optometry schools have students doing patient encounters during year three. Take advantage of clinical rotations and exposure to diverse patient populations to develop a broader understanding of ocular conditions, treatment plans, and overall optometric care.

Financial Tip

Gain access to EyeDock PRO for FREE via the Student Ambassador Program. EyeDock PRO is the largest online clinical database/tool for any clinical questions you may have.

Cultivate Non-Clinical Knowledge

Most private practice owners will say that clinical expertise doesn't amount to much in the real world if the bills aren't getting paid. In other words, book smarts alone don't lead to revenue generation if other items are not taken into consideration—mainly billing and coding (B&C).

Begin to understand how the clinical care you provide for patients impacts income for a practice. Seek advice from preceptors who also work in private practice. Join the ODs on Finance group and ask questions. Read B&C articles in optometric journals. Having a confident B&C knowledge base will also help you stand out in the job search process.

Financial Tip

Patient communication is a crucial non-textbook skill that can be the sole difference between being an average or an exceptional eye care provider. Develop and nurture your ability to effectively and efficiently communicate with patients with each clinical encounter you take on.

Don't Make a Spectacle of Yourself

I am as much in favor of optometric scope expansion as the hard-core advocates. However, we must not lose touch with our ability to improve patients' lives through visual correction. Do not lose sight of the fact that the majority of patients present for eye examinations because they want clearer vision. It is your job to help patients gain this positive experience. What good will knowing about the newest pipeline presbyopia medication do if 25 percent of your patients are coming in for spectacle prescription checks?

Now is the time to hone your refraction skills and familiarize yourself with different spectacle lens technologies—progressive addition lenses, anti-fatigue lenses, computer bifocals, etc. I can assure you that practice owners would be pleased to learn that you've taken time to learn about different lens options that will help patients experience sharper and more comfortable vision.

Embrace Leadership Opportunities

Look for opportunities to take on leadership roles within your optometry school. Join student associations, committees, or clubs that align with your interests. Most schools have a variety of organizations that may pique your interest—including private practice clubs, Beta Sigma Kappa, Fellowship of Christian Optometrists, contact lens clubs, and more. These experiences can enhance your leadership skills and allow you an opportunity to make a positive impact. Lastly, consider spending time assisting with a VOSH trip. You won't regret it!

Prepare for Licensure Exams

The third year is when the preparation for board examinations ramps up as NBEO Part 1 looms around the corner. Familiarize yourself with the format and content of the exams, and consider utilizing study resources and review courses. Develop a study plan and allocate dedicated time to review and practice exam-style questions. Be sure to have a dedicated test-taking plan set *prior* to taking boards instead of just "winging it!"

Cultivate Professional Relationships

From this point on, networking and building professional relationships will be a crucial component of your career journey. Attend optometry conferences to connect with industry professionals and students from other schools. Make friends. Seek out mentors. Connect with people who can provide guidance as you prepare to enter the workforce. Furthermore, don't simply accumulate business cards to store in a drawer after meetings. Make *meaningful* connections and follow up appropriately. Consider getting business cards of your own and making them unique. First impressions are important!

Financial Tip

Many exhibit halls at major optometry conferences accommodate a photography booth. Carve out some time to get a (free) professional headshot to update your resume/CV and social media profiles.

Explore Research or Other Degree Opportunities

If research interests you, consider pursuing research projects during your third year. Moreover, some optometry institutions have Master of Science or PhD degrees that allow an opportunity to go above and beyond the typical optometric education to emphasize research curriculum and training. Engaging in research deepens your understanding of a specific area of vision or the eyes and grants you the occasion to contribute to the advancement of the field. If lecturing and publishing are of interest to you, consider obtaining a graduate degree, as it could open more doors for professional development.

Consider Career Settings

Optometric employment opportunities are abundant. Something to ask yourself is whether you want a job or a career position. Would you be happy in a retail setting? Could you experience burnout in an ophthalmology office? Do you want to learn about the business side of optometry in a private practice? Is performing research in an academic setting of interest to you?

In addition to exploring different optometric work settings, you should begin to narrow down potential geographic living areas. The general pros and cons of urban versus rural living are well-established. Metropolitan areas offer more in the way of culture, cuisine, and activities. However, saturated markets tend to result in lower optometric salaries. On the contrary, rural areas are less known for their diversity, music festivals, and nightlife but usually outcompete cities in terms of optometrist compensation and scope of practice. We won't get into other urban versus rural differences with respect to more complex topics such as race, faith, and more.

Which setting and region suit you best?

Begin Thinking of a Residency

Residency training can be a wonderful experience for many of our colleagues. At the same time, it is not required for the vast majority of employment opportunities for optometrists. Whether you ultimately decide to pursue a residency position or not, the third year of optometry school is when you should begin considering if a residency may be the right option for you. Refer to chapter 9 for more information on residencies.

The third year of optometry school is not without challenges, but it's also the stage where becoming a doctor starts to feel more realistic. Stay committed, seek opportunities for growth, and remember to take care of yourself throughout this exciting phase of your education.

Year 4

As you enter your fourth and final year of optometry school, congratulations are in order! You've come a long way in your journey to becoming a doctor. Now it's time to focus on honing your clinical expertise and preparing for a successful transition into professional practice. Here's how to make the most of your final year:

Refine Examination Skills

Focus on refining and perfecting your clinical acumen. Improve your slit lamp technique. Get more comfortable using a BIO. Improve refraction speed and efficiency. Actively seek out the more complex cases.

Opt for the most challenging clinical rotations and learn how to provide high-quality patient care under the guidance of experienced ODs. Take advantage of feedback and guidance from faculty and supervisors to continue improving your skills.

Importantly, do not solely focus on examination techniques at the expense of improving communication ability. The smartest physician in the room does NOT always equate to the best physician if interpersonal skills are lacking. Work on delivering unfortunate news to patients and families, explaining ocular conditions simply, expressing treatment plans to ensure adequate compliance, and more. We cannot understate the extreme importance that developing your presentation and communication skills will play in your career success.

Prepare for Board Examinations

Ultimately, you will not be practicing as an optometrist without passing boards. It is essential to prepare for the board examinations appropriately by familiarizing yourself with the exam format, content, and timelines. Seek support and advice from classmates and friends who have already gone through the process. Sign up for board preparation materials offered by a couple of well-known exam prep companies. Most of all, STUDY AND PRACTICE!

Stay the Course

Persist in the pursuit of personal and professional development. Continue attending conferences, building your network, and taking care of your physical and mental self. The finish line is near!

Build a Professional Network

Networking becomes even more crucial in your final year as you prepare to enter the optometry profession. Contacts may be able to connect you with potential employers for career opportunities. Develop AND maintain relationships with mentors and preceptors who can provide guidance and support during your transition to professional practice.

Complete Clinical Externships

Take advantage of fourth-year clinical rotations to gain real-world exposure and improve your clinical skills in different practice settings. These externships provide valuable hands-on experience and may even lead to job opportunities after graduation. Actively engage with patients, ask questions, and seek feedback from supervising clinicians.

Importantly, begin to familiarize yourself with the different contact lens manufacturers and their products. Ask preceptors about their preferred contact lens devices and *why* that is so. Learn about the nuances in different designs, fitting modalities, parameter and material options, and how it all comes together to give patients an overall positive contact lens experience. In addition, delve into the world of spectacle lens products and the different technologies and designs available. Become accustomed to making clinically appropriate visual recommendations to patients in the exam room. Patients expect you to be the expert in ocular health *and* vision correction. Prove them right.

Billing and Coding

Here is a very common and unfortunate position that many new optometrists find themselves in after graduation. You've landed an awesome job, and you're ecstatic about beginning your career as a doctor. Your first day of clinic is off to a wonderful start, and it comes time to complete an eye examination on your first patient outside of optometry school. What a long way you've come!

You finish the evaluation and come across the last documentation section in the chart—*billing and coding*. And then you realize . . . you're not sure how to properly assign a diagnosis and procedural code(s) to the patient exam. Oh no!

Try to avoid this uncomfortable situation by making a concerted effort to enlighten yourself on billing and coding principles during the fourth year of optometry school (and hopefully in previous years as well). Billing and coding is a nebulous topic, and the reality is that even many seasoned ODs don't have a good understanding of how to accurately think through assigning diagnostic and procedural codes to patient encounters.

To address this, be sure to ask preceptors, read optometric business articles, take online continuing education courses, and peruse recommended books to improve your ability to hit the ground running in your first job after graduation.

Think Beyond the Exam Lane

Associate ODs generally want to improve their income. Practice owners enjoy taking home more money. **What's one way for all parties to get what they each desire?** Increase revenue generation by associate optometrists!

One of the most misunderstood topics for optometry students and new grads is how a practice generates revenue. It really is too much to cover in this book, but an optometry clinic can produce money from a variety of outlets, including professional fees (i.e., eye examinations, contact lens fittings), optical sales (i.e., glasses and contact lenses), special testing (i.e., OCT scans, visual fields, retinal imaging), and other miscellaneous goods (i.e., nutraceuticals, warm compresses, artificial tears). A great associate can maximize these opportunities each and every clinic day to improve the overall profitability of a practice.

Do some research and speak with colleagues about all that goes into becoming a high-producing associate OD and steps that you can take to optimize production, such as developing strong "sale from the chair" skills, increasing patient volume, expanding upon cash-pay specialty eye care services, and more.

Importantly, the care that we provide always comes first, and doctors should never prioritize profits over patients. At the same time, we have to get comfortable with the idea that we don't have to live as martyrs. It is OKAY to want to improve income for yourself and your business. Doing so not only improves your take-home pay but also enhances the opportunity to reinvest in the practice (i.e., new equipment), expand services to improve clinical care, and offer better wages to staff to improve the lives of their families. There is not a practice owner in the country who would not want their associate to maximize income.

Financial Tip

Remember that the gross (overall) revenue produced in a clinic does NOT equate to what a practice owner takes home. There are many expenses involved in running an office that chip away at the "top line revenue," including cost of goods sold, staff wages, rent, utilities, equipment debt, and more. Subtracting expenses from the gross dollars results in net revenue.

Navigate the Job Search Process

Seeking employment can be a rigorous and competitive process. Apply for jobs using the various optometric career search portals online, including ODs on Finance Careers. Take time to prepare for job interviews to help you stand out from other applicants and secure a coveted position. You have accumulated academic knowledge and developed hands-on clinical experience. Articulating this expertise confidently, understanding the employer's practice, mission, and values, and demonstrating your readiness to contribute to the clinic can leave a positive impression on a hiring party. Flip the interview script and focus on what you can do for the employer, not what the employer can do for you.

Prepare for the Transition to Practice

Graduation marks the transition from optometry student to practicing optometrist. Begin planning for this transition early on by researching career opportunities. Develop a professional curriculum vitae (CV) and/or resume, and be sure to update your online presence (such as LinkedIn).

Solidify your decision on whether or not to apply for a residency position. Many fourth-year students even take the leap and cold start or purchase a practice.

One of the wonderful things about optometry is there is no shortage of work settings—corporate/retail, sublease, private practice, ophthalmology office, residency position, hospital, VA institution, academia, refractive surgery center, reservation, correctional facility, and more. Each practice setting comes with its own pros and cons. The opportunities are endless!

Plan Ahead

The fourth year of optometry school is the time to narrow down which state you would like to practice in. It is important to enlighten yourself about the specific licensing requirements where you want to live, as they can vary from state to state.

Celebrate Your Achievements

Completing your final year is an accomplishment worth celebrating. Take a moment to appreciate what you've done and how far you've come. For many of us, the journey is a struggle— a daily grind. Fortunately, the final outcome is worth it. After graduation, continue to improve as a clinician and a person, provide great care to patients, and be a steadfast bastion for our profession in the years to come.

Closing Thoughts

Optometry school is like a roller coaster ride. There are ups and downs, and it can be exciting at times, as well as frightening. Our hope is that by carefully reading through these excerpts and, more importantly, *actually* implementing them, you'll be better prepared to tackle your educational journey and the adventures that follow. Develop good habits, work hard, get outside of your comfort zone, meet new people, practice your clinical skills, seek challenging opportunities, plan ahead, and stay curious. We all have more to learn. We all have room to grow. Let's do so together.

Key Takeaways:

- Optometry school is not just about academic excellence but also about holistic career preparation. As students transition through the years, they should equip themselves with a range of skills, insights, and experiences that lay the foundation for their future careers.

- While clinical expertise is paramount, understanding the business side of optometry, such as billing and coding, is equally crucial. Additionally, soft skills like patient communication can differentiate an average optometrist from an exceptional one.

- Building a professional network early on, especially during the more relaxed years, can open doors to job opportunities and mentorship later. This includes attending conferences, joining student associations, and actively participating in extracurricular activities.

- The final year is about refining clinical skills, navigating the job search process, and preparing for the transition from student to practicing optometrist. This involves planning for state-specific licensing requirements, updating professional profiles, and celebrating the journey's achievements.

PART III

THE NEW GRAD—NEXT STEPS FOR FINANCIAL FREEDOM

CHAPTER 12:

INVESTING BASICS FOR THE OPTOMETRY STUDENT | BY DAT BUI, OD

> Investing should be more like watching paint dry
> or watching grass grow. If you want excitement,
> take $800 and go to Las Vegas.
> **—Paul Samuelson**

During a recent reunion, I met up with Tiffany, one of my smartest classmates from optometry school. She was doing exceptionally well in California, working at a renowned private office. Naturally, our conversation veered toward personal finance. I began talking about index funds, tax-efficient retirement strategies, and the like.

But to my surprise, Tiffany interrupted, revealing she hadn't ventured into investing at all, feeling it was too complex. Instead, she parked all her money in a savings account. Despite being a top performer in our optometry class, the world of investments seemed to intimidate her.

It's a common misconception; many students believe investing is this complex maze reserved for finance wizards. However, in reality, it's a crucial step for long-term financial stability and is more accessible than most think.

Forget the hectic Wall Street scenes you've pictured with brokers screaming "BUY!" or "SELL!" Everyday investing is more like a peaceful garden—it's all about patience and letting things grow at their own pace.

Investing can be as intricate or as straightforward as you desire. If you've navigated the rigorous path of optometry school, then trust me, you can easily get the hang of investing!

Today's investment landscape is transforming. With digital platforms like Vanguard or Fidelity offering passive low-cost index funds, and the rise of robo-advisers such as Betterment and Wealthfront, the era of high-fee managed funds and expensive financial advisors is over. Most of us, especially in the medical field, are perfectly capable of managing our own investments without hefty fees.

Of course, if you wish to delve deeper or explore various investing strategies later on, there's a plethora of resources available, including books and online courses. In our discussions, we'll frequently refer to Vanguard index funds due to their cost-effectiveness. Still, there are other reputable platforms like Fidelity, Charles Schwab, or E-Trade to consider.

In a nutshell, don't let the initial fear of the unknown deter you from the world of investing. Just like in optometry, with a bit of knowledge and the right tools, you can excel.

While we recognize that optometry students often have tight finances and might not have spare money to invest, acquiring financial literacy early on is crucial for your future success as a doctor. With that in mind, in six concise sections, we will cover the following:

    i.   **The Basics: Essentials of Investing and Investing Terms**

    ii.   **Building the Perfect Portfolio: A Mix of Stocks and Bonds**

    iii.   **Strategies for Rebalancing Asset Allocation & Exploring Other Asset Classes**

    iv.   **A Quick Guide to Assessing Mutual or Index Funds**

    v.   **The Era of Target Date Retirement Funds and Robo-Advisers: Choosing the Right Brokerage**

    vi.   **Tracking Investment Performance and Other Wealth-Building Insights**

(I) The Basics: The Essentials of Investing and Investing Terms

First, let's delve into the concept of *investment* and explore its various risk levels, ranging from basic savings accounts to the volatile world of cryptocurrencies.

According to the Merriam-Webster dictionary, an *investment* is defined as "the allocation of money with the expectation of obtaining income or profit." In today's context, the term *investment* is frequently employed, sometimes to the point of overuse and occasional misuse.

Investments:	Not an investments:
<ul><li>Stocks</li><li>Bonds</li><li>Mutual funds</li><li>Exchange-traded funds (ETFs)</li><li>Businesses</li><li>Real estate</li><li>Hedge funds</li><li>Private equity</li><li>Rare materials with high demand relative to supply</li></ul>	<ul><li>Currencies, e.g., the Yen</li><li>Cryptocurrencies like Bitcoin</li><li>Multi-level marketing (MLM) ventures</li><li>Your primary residence</li><li>Vehicles and collectible items, like baseball cards</li><li>Household appliances</li><li>Gambling or lottery endeavors</li></ul>

While none of the items under the "Not Investments" side of the chart have intrinsic value as we have defined above, remember that certain items can be used to make money (and subsequently lose money), such as crypto-currency or gambling. However, they do not qualify for our traditional definition of an investment. These items are based **mostly on speculation and chance,** rather than their ability to generate income.

Okay, let's start with some basic investing terminology so we can have a solid foundation and understand investing lingo. *Don't worry, it won't be as bad as neuro-anatomy.*

What Is a Stock?

A *stock* represents shares of ownership in a company, sometimes referred to as *equity*. There are numerous ways to own a company's stock or stocks of multiple companies. For instance, by purchasing an S&P 500 index, you can share in the profits (and losses) of a specific company, such as Apple.

There are four primary ways to own stock:

1) **Individual Stock Purchase**

   Purchasing individual stocks entails purchasing shares of a specific company via a brokerage. This strategy has inherent risks since you're investing in a single company. This type of investing has the allure of the company becoming the next big success, like trying to find the next Apple or Amazon, but it also has the potential for a downfall, akin to Enron in 2008. Investing in individual stocks demands significant research, staying updated with financial reports and current events, and a higher risk appetite. Most 401(k) plans don't allow buying individual stocks due to the associated high risk.

   ### Financial Tip

   For the majority of investors, **both novices and seasoned ones, we advise AGAINST individual stocks** They're NOT a prerequisite for investment success. We advocate for low-cost, passive stock index funds as the backbone of their portfolios. Stick to this, and you'll fare well! If the idea of picking stocks intrigues you, we suggest allocating no more than 10 percent of your portfolio.

2) Mutual Funds

Think of a mutual fund as a diversified basket containing a variety of investments such as stocks, bonds, or specific asset classes like real estate or technology.

Some funds even exclusively invest in ethical or environmentally conscious companies. What's the appeal of a mutual fund? With a single transaction, you get a diverse collection of investments, enabling immediate, effortless diversification. This spares you the task of buying stocks individually. The fund is under the active management of a professional, usually for a fee ranging from 0.25 percent to potentially 2.5 percent.

3) Index Fund

Purchasing stock within an index or as part of a mutual fund is typically the safest stock ownership method. We highly recommend cost-effective, passive index funds such as the total stock index fund or the S&P 500 index fund. They're very affordable, around 0.03 percent, and the average ten-year return for the stock index is roughly 10 percent. Numerous indices exist, tracking everything from technology to real estate. However, the S&P 500 index is among the most popular.

4) Exchange-Traded Funds (ETFs)

ETFs are gaining immense popularity. Much like index funds, they are passive and low-cost. Yet they offer a broader spectrum of specific indices, allowing investments in specialized sectors like healthcare. Plus, ETFs can be bought, sold, or traded anytime during market hours, akin to individual stocks. The beauty of an ETF lies in its accessibility. As they're traded like stocks, investors can buy them at smaller share prices, often below the sizable minimum investments many mutual funds demand—making them an ideal choice for beginners such as optometry students.

Example

Consider the Vanguard S&P 500 Index Admiral mutual fund (VFIAX) requiring a minimum of $3,000. It may not be feasible for some new investors. Therefore, they provide the Vanguard S&P 500 ETF (VOO), offering similar returns but available at a per-share price.

What Is a Bond?

In essence, bonds represent portions of loans given to companies or governments, but are part of a larger borrowed sum. Bond maturities can vary from one to twenty-five years. The borrower, such as the US government, agrees to repay the loan with interest, which is where the profit comes in. The average bond return is about 2–3 percent. Bonds are often low yield and deemed "safe."

Their primary role? To dampen portfolio volatility during market downturns. Much like the total stock index, we suggest a straightforward, low-cost, passive total bond market index fund.

Understanding Key Financial Terms:

What Is an Expense Ratio?

This is the annual charge, usually a percentage, that mutual or index funds impose on investors for management. It covers management and operational administrative costs. This is paramount because it directly affects your profit. Note that this is over and above a typical financial advising fee (AUM) of 1–2 percent if you opt for a financial advisor.

Example

An actively managed mutual fund might have an expense ratio of 1.80 percent, while a passive index fund could charge as low as 0.02 percent.

What Is Asset Allocation?

Asset allocation refers to the composition of your investment portfolio. Assets can be diverse, from stocks and bonds to commodities like gold or silver. Most investors primarily hold stocks and bonds. For instance, a young investor in their late twenties or early thirties might have 90 percent in stocks and 10 percent in bonds. Stock investments come in varied forms, which we'll delve deeper into later.

Why Are Low-Cost & Passive Stock Index Funds (ETF) the Best Investment Route?

Warren Buffet famously stated, "By periodically investing in a low-cost broad-market index fund like the S&P 500 index, the know-nothing investor can actually outperform most investment professionals." Index funds, steered by algorithms, aim to mirror market behavior. Conversely, actively managed mutual funds that strive to exceed market returns often underperform, especially after accounting for fees.

Let's Review 5 Reasons Why a Passive Index Fund Is the Best Investment:

1) **Cost efficiency:** Passive index funds have a low fee, approximately 0.09 percent, in comparison to the higher fees of actively managed funds, which hover around 0.78 percent.

2) **Superior performance:** Research indicates that over a span of ten years, an index fund outperforms nearly 80 percent of actively managed funds when fees are taken into account. The beauty of an index fund is its alignment with the market. If the market surges by 28 percent, your fund benefits. And if it drops by 10 percent, there's no need for panic as the entire market faces a similar decline.

3) **Tax efficiency:** The low turnover rate within an index fund translates to fewer capital gains distributions. This, in turn, means reduced tax liabilities for investors.

4) **Time savings**: Opting for an index fund means there's no need to dive deep into research, keeping tabs on individual stocks, or monitoring specific companies. Especially for professionals like doctors, time can be more productively utilized, whether it's attending to patients or enhancing our practices.

5) **Minimized risk:** Investing in an index fund curtails many potential pitfalls an investor might face. For instance, the temptation to pursue a stock, envisioning it to be the next Apple, is curbed. An index fund inherently diversifies your investment across the market, reducing the risk of concentrating too much capital in a single stock.

It's essential to understand that financial jargon, akin to terms in eye anatomy, has its unique lexicon. By mastering these terms, you'll be better positioned as an investor, enabling you to sophisticate your portfolio as you see fit.

The Art of Proper Asset Allocation

Determining the right asset allocation can be the most crucial, and often the most stressful, decision an investor makes for their retirement or other taxable investment accounts. Many investors spend a lot of unnecessary time on this step, resulting in stress. However, whether your asset allocation is simple or complex, it can still serve you well.

Our recommendation? Keep it simple. Believe it or not, even the most successful investor might have a portfolio comprising just three to five funds.

Follow these 3 basic steps to devise an ideal asset allocation strategy:

STEP 1) Decide on the Percentage of Stocks vs. Bonds:

Each investor's choice varies, influenced by individual personality and risk tolerance. The higher your risk tolerance, the more stocks should dominate your portfolio.

Here's a scenario: If you have $500,000 invested entirely in stocks and the market plummets by 50 percent (resembling the 2008-09 crash), could you bear a $250,000 loss, waiting four to five years for recovery? If this gives you pause, consider a heavier bond allocation.

Also, reflect on when you'll actually need the funds—likely around retirement. Most investments are considered long term (beyond five years), as this duration allows the market ample time for recovery. Remember, for many, it wasn't until 2012 that they recouped their losses from the 2008 debacle.

Financial Tip

A good rule of thumb for long-term investing: as retirement nears, incrementally shift your portfolio toward bonds. Imagine the repercussions of a significant market crash when you're a year shy of retirement with a fully stock-weighted portfolio. Such an event could necessitate additional working years for financial recovery.

For determining the stock-bond ratio, age can be instructive. A thirty-year-old might lean toward a 90–10 stock-bond ratio, while a sixty-year-old might prefer a 60–40 split due to impending retirement.

Recommended Stock to Bond Ratio (Age Range)		
AGE	AMOUNT OF BONDS %	AMOUNT OF STOCKS %
20-30	0 %	100%
30-40	10%	90%
40-50	20%	80%
50-60	30%	70%
> 60	40%	60%

For young investors in their twenties or early thirties, even a 100 percent stock portfolio could be fitting. Though high in risk, with a clear understanding and the right mindset, it can promise rewarding long-term returns.

Which Bond Fund to Pick?

The Vanguard Total Bond Market Index Fund is a popular choice. This comprehensive bond index boasts an impressively low expense ratio of 0.15 percent. Its ten-year average gain is a modest 3.5 percent, just enough to outpace annual inflation. As you grow in investment expertise, you might explore other bond types, but starting simple is always a smart move.

Financial Tip

If you are a young investor in your twenties or early thirties and you want to do a 100 percent stock portfolio, that is perfectly okay! I know plenty of young investors who have all stock portfolios because they want the highest return yield. Overall, the Vanguard Total Stock Market Index Fund has a return of 10.5 percent over a fifteen-year course.

STEP 2) Within the Stock Portfolio, Which Types of Stocks Should I Invest In?

Domestic US stocks should be the cornerstone, making up roughly 75 percent of your allocation. Given the robustness of the US economy, this is where significant returns are anticipated.

There's variability, of course: the US Total Stock Index soared by 33 percent in 2013 but also plummeted by 37 percent in the 2008 downturn. Over a fifteen-year period, however, the average return stands around an appealing 10.5 percent.

US Domestic Stocks vs. International Stocks:

US domestic stock funds are tied to US-based giants like Amazon. In contrast, international stock funds reach across borders, from Alibaba in China to Volkswagen in Europe. Allocating a modest 25 percent of your stock portfolio to international stocks can diversify your holdings. However, is it essential? Not really. One can make the argument that any US corporation has significant global operations, inadvertently giving you international exposure.

Large-Cap vs. Mid-Cap vs. Small-Cap Stocks:

A fund's capitalization size indicates its realm of investment. Large-cap funds focus on behemoths like Apple, mid-cap funds on names like Guess, and small-cap funds might delve into lesser-known entities such as Spectrum Pharmaceuticals. Generally, large-cap funds, leaning on major US companies, promise stability, albeit potentially with modest returns. Conversely, small-cap funds, targeting nimble, emerging entities, come with elevated risks but potentially stellar returns. Mid-cap offers a balanced mix.

Now, with a clearer grasp of stock types, you're better positioned to make informed asset allocation decisions.

(II) Building the Perfect Portfolio: A Mix of Stocks and Bonds

4 Portfolio Asset Allocation Examples:

Now that you understand the basic stock types, let's delve into stock allocation.

Let's assume a young, thirty-year-old doctor-investor wants a 100 percent stock portfolio, setting aside the bond portion for now. What might their stock fund profile look like?

For our examples, we'll utilize Vanguard index ETF funds. It's essential to note that an ETF version of an index fund mirrors its counterpart, but the former allows for the purchase of smaller amounts. This feature is especially beneficial for new investors who may not have substantial funds. The following four passive-index, low-cost stock funds should form the core of your portfolio:

- **Vanguard Total Stock Market Index Fund ETF (VTI):** Captures the performance of all company stocks in the USA.

- **Vanguard S&P 500 ETF (VOO):** Reflects the performance of the top five hundred stocks in the USA, mainly large-cap with a smattering of mid-cap companies.

- **Vanguard Small-Cap Index Fund ETF (VB):** Monitors the performance of all small-cap company stocks in the USA.

- **Vanguard Total International Stock Index Fund ETF (VXUS):** Tracks the performance of international stocks outside the USA.

For our bond fund, we'll utilize a straightforward, low-cost index bond fund ETF, which is the **Vanguard Total Bond Market Index Fund ETF (BND).**

Here are four simple yet effective portfolio examples, suitable for investors ranging from beginners to experts. Remember that the objective behind each portfolio is to diversify your assets and ensure exposure across different segments.

ODs on Finance	Portfolio #1	Portfolio #2	Portfolio #3	Portfolio #4
25% of total Stock	Vanguard Total Stock Market Stock Index		Vanguard Total Stock Market Stock Index	Vanguard Total Stock Market Stock Index
25% of total Stock	Vanguard S&P 500 Stock Index			--------or--------
25% of total Stock	Vanguard Small Cap Stock Index	Vanguard Small Cap Stock Index		Vanguard S&P 500 Stock Index
25% of total Stock	Vanguard Total International Stock Index	Vanguard Total International Stock Index	Vanguard Total International Stock Index	

> **+ Plus Vanguard Total Bond Market Index Fund**
> **(Whatever % of total portfolio that you devote to Bond)**

Portfolio #1: It employs a straightforward strategy, allocating 25 percent to each major fund for balanced exposure. The returns of both the Total Stock Market and the S&P 500 funds are similar, but at least one or both should form the cornerstone of any portfolio.

Portfolio #2: Half of its assets are tied to the S&P 500 fund, which focuses mainly on large-cap and some mid-cap companies. To achieve a broader spectrum of exposure, it's wise to also invest in a small-cap stock fund, effectively tilting the portfolio toward smaller companies.

Portfolio #3: This portfolio essentially merges the S&P 500 and the Small-Cap Index into the Total Stock Market fund, granting us exposure across all stock tiers: large, mid, and small.

Portfolio #4: One might wonder about the rationale behind Portfolio #4 since it lacks direct international exposure. However, remember that a significant portion of US companies operate globally, which indirectly exposes us to international markets. So if an investor leans toward exclusively US stocks, that's a perfectly valid choice.

In essence, similar to refraction, asset allocation is both an art and a science. Each of these portfolios possesses unique merits and strengths, ensuring ample diversification. Many investors prefer simplicity and a minimalistic approach, making Portfolio #3 or #4 particularly appealing. Whichever allocation you choose, you're poised for success. And as you broaden your financial understanding, you can always embrace a more intricate portfolio structure.

(III) Strategies for Rebalancing Asset Allocation & Exploring Other Asset Classes

Rebalance Your Asset Allocation Each Year

Imagine you started 2019 with 70 percent of your portfolio in stock mutual funds and 30 percent in bonds. By year's end, due to market fluctuations, you might find yourself with 75 percent in stocks and 25 percent in bonds. In such a case, rebalancing means adjusting back to your original 70 percent–30 percent allocation. Some investors rebalance more frequently, such as monthly (which can be excessive) or when they hit a certain threshold (like 40 percent stock).

However, we advise simplicity: **rebalancing ONCE A YEAR is generally sufficient**. Numerous 401(k) or IRA accounts offer features that enable investors to set the percentage of their mutual funds to a desired stock/bond ratio, streamlining the rebalancing process.

Bear in mind, the more asset classes (like commodities or REITs) or multiple IRA accounts you hold, the more intricate the process becomes.

Financial Tip

Rebalancing your portfolio simply means correcting any imbalances, restoring your original stock-to-bond ratio. It's advisable to keep it uncomplicated: rebalance ONCE A YEAR.

Additional Asset Classes

Here's a quick rundown of other investments you might consider for your portfolio. Do these asset classes guarantee success? No! But as you advance in your investing journey and seek diversification, these could be of interest. Typically, a modest 5–10 percent allocation to these alternative investments is what we recommend:

1. Emerging Market
2. REIT (Real Estate Trust) Funds
3. Commodities Fund
4. Sector Funds
5. Individual Stocks

(1) Emerging Markets Mutual Funds:

These funds concentrate on companies in developing or emerging countries, such as Brazil and, perhaps surprisingly, China. While these nations aren't underdeveloped, they aren't fully developed either, often resulting in accelerated growth (and potentially higher returns) than established US Domestic companies. **The catch? They are extremely volatile.**

These markets can experience dramatic fluctuations in a short span. Many investors opt for a maximum of 10 percent allocation to emerging markets to strike a balance between risk and reward.

Recommended: Vanguard Emerging Markets Index ETF Shares (VWO)

(2) REIT (Real Estate Investment Trust) Funds:

If real estate piques your interest but you lack the resources or inclination to buy properties or be a landlord, then REITs provide an avenue. They invest in a range of real estate properties, from commercial to residential. They aren't essential but can diversify your portfolio.

Financial Tip

Due to their mandatory dividend payouts each earning period, REITs can be tax inefficient. It's best to hold them in tax-deferred retirement accounts like Roth IRAs or 401(k)s.

Recommended: Vanguard Real Estate Index ETF (VNQ)

(3) Commodities Fund:

Such funds invest in goods like agricultural produce, natural resources, and precious metals. They generally offer low returns and might not be the best long-term investments. Avoid straightforward commodities like gold or weed (even though it lowers IOP), as they don't generate tangible products. For instance, from 1836 to 2011, gold's inflation-adjusted return was a paltry 1.1 percent. If keen on precious metals, consider commodity index funds or stocks of companies that leverage these commodities.

Recommended: Vanguard Materials Index Fund ETF (VAW)

(4) Sector Funds:

These funds invest exclusively in businesses within specific industry sectors, such as technology or healthcare. They can be structured as mutual funds or ETFs. If a particular sector aligns with your interests or expertise (e.g., healthcare for doctors), sector index funds are an efficient choice. However, be aware that these funds often come with higher management fees.

Recommended: Vanguard Information Technology Index ETF (VGT), Vanguard Financials Index ETF (VFH), Vanguard Utilities Index ETF (VPU), Vanguard Health Care Index ETF (VHT), Vanguard Consumer Staples Index ETF (VDC), Vanguard Communication Services Index (VOX).

(5) What About Individual Stocks?

You might be pondering, *"What about individual stocks? That is all my rich doctor buddies talk about?"* Investing in particular companies, like Apple or Tesla, is exciting but higher risk. It demands comprehensive research into the company's financial history, earnings reports, and future prospects. To excel as an individual stock investor, you must critically determine the company's value and fundamentals and stay updated with its current events and quarterly reports. This can be a source of significant stress for novice investors. But if you strike gold by investing in the next Google or Apple, the returns can be immense!

Please note that it is nearly impossible to beat the market return of an S&P 500 index market return over the long term, even for the most experienced professional asset managers.

However, as your investing acumen grows and you feel the urge to explore individual stocks, go for it! They can enhance your portfolio's diversity and boost potential earnings. That said, individual stocks aren't for everyone, and they're NOT a prerequisite for investment success. For most, we advocate for low-cost, passive stock index funds as the backbone of their portfolios. Stick to this, and you'll fare well!

Buffett's Bet on Index Funds vs. Hedge Funds

In 2007, Warren Buffett challenged the hedge fund industry, betting that a simple S&P 500 index fund would outperform a selection of hedge funds over a decade. Asset management firm Protege Partners took the challenge, selecting five fund-of-funds to compete against Buffett's choice. By the end of 2017, the index fund had an average annual return of 7.1 percent, while the hedge funds managed about 2.2 percent. Buffett's win highlighted the value of low-cost, passive investing over the high fees of active hedge fund management.

(IV) A Quick Guide To Assessing Mutual Or Index Funds

5 Steps to Assess a Mutual or Index Fund:

As a budding optometrist starting your first job, you'll likely access an employer-sponsored 401(k). Glancing at your 401(k)'s mutual fund options might initially feel overwhelming. Here's a streamlined guide to assessing a mutual fund in under a minute:

1. **Identify funds matching your asset allocation:**

    Although we've frequently cited Vanguard, major brokerage firms like Fidelity offer similar funds. Most 401(k) plans feature mutual funds resembling a Total Stock Market Index Fund.

    Example: Fidelity Total Stock Market Index Fund (FSKAX) is akin to Vanguard Total Stock Market Index Fund (VTSMX) in cost and return.

2. **Input the fund's ticker symbol:**

    We recommend Yahoo Finance, but MorningStar is also another great resource (both are free). It unveils the asset types the fund concentrates on, such as Stock vs Bond, or Large-cap vs Small-cap companies.

    Example: Vanguard Mid-Cap Index fund, symbolized by VO, primarily invests in mid-cap US stocks.

3. **Opt for no-load funds:**

    Avoid funds that impose extra fees (sometimes as high as 5 percent) for purchase. These fees might be charged upfront (FRONT-loaded) or after a period (BACK-loaded). On Yahoo Finance, a "NONE" under the "load option" indicates a no-load fund.

4. Prioritize a low expense ratio:

This key determinant can significantly affect your long-term earnings. Many low-cost, passive index funds feature ratios below 0.10 percent; some are even around 0.05 percent. Steer clear of actively managed funds, which can carry heftier ratios. In constrained choices, aim for an expense ratio under 1 percent.

5. Review past performance:

While past achievements don't guarantee future outcomes, they offer a glimpse of patterns. Examine first, third, and tenth-year performances for a holistic view.

Example: As of 2023, the Vanguard Total Stock Market Index (VTI) performed at:

- One year = 12.59 percent
- Three years = 13 percent
- Ten years = 12.07 percent

Refrain from being overly swayed by a 12.59 percent gain; it's an exception. An average 8.60 percent return over a decade offers a more pragmatic long-term projection. As you hone your investment skills, you can delve deeper, but this foundational knowledge suffices for swift fund assessment.

How to Analyze a Fund + Compare Good vs Bad:

Let's delve into a comparison between two stocks that track the Total Stock Market. On the surface, they may seem similar in assets, but as we'll discover, fees and hidden costs can transform one into a less-than-desirable investment option.

We'll look at the following:

- **Vanguard Total Stock Market Index Investor Shares (VTSMX)**

- **Invesco Oppenheimer Main Street (MSIGX)**

Example #1: Vanguard Total Stock Market Index Fund Investor Shares (VTSMX)

Let's say that you come across the Vanguard Total Stock Market Index Fund Investor Shares (VTSMX) within your 401(k) and want to delve deeper. Using Yahoo Finance, simply input the VTSMX ticker into the search bar.

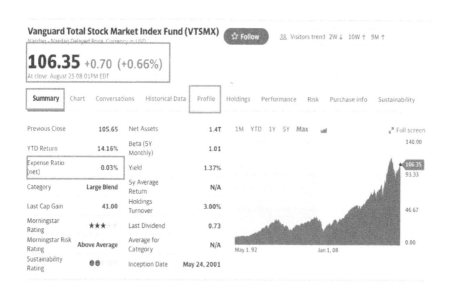

Summary:

- **Current price per share:** $106.35 (This isn't a pivotal metric.)

- **Expense ratio (cost of fund):** At a mere 0.03 percent annually, this is notably cheap, a trait of index funds.

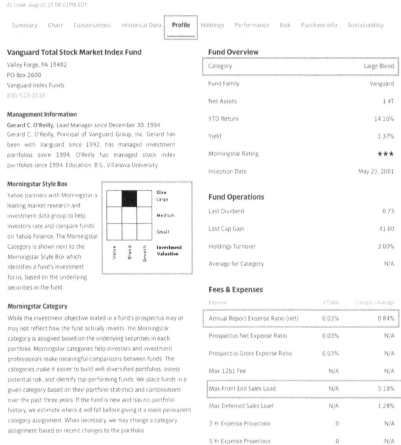

106.35 +0.70 (+0.66%)
At close: August 25 08 01PM EDT

Summary   Chart   Conversations   Historical Data   **Profile**   Holdings   Performance   Risk   Purchase info   Sustainability

Vanguard Total Stock Market Index Fund

Valley Forge, PA 19482
PO Box 2600
Vanguard Index Funds
800-523-1036

Management Information

Gerard C. O'Reilly, Lead Manager since December 30, 1994
Gerard C. O'Reilly, Principal of Vanguard Group, Inc. Gerard has been with Vanguard since 1992, has managed investment portfolios since 1994. O'Reilly has managed stock index portfolios since 1994. Education: B.S., Villanova University.

Morningstar Style Box

Yahoo partners with Morningstar a leading market research and investment data group to help investors rate and compare funds on Yahoo Finance. The Morningstar Category is shown next to the Morningstar Style Box which identifies a fund's investment focus, based on the underlying securities in the fund.

Morningstar Category

While the investment objective stated in a fund's prospectus may or may not reflect how the fund actually invests, the Morningstar category is assigned based on the underlying securities in each portfolio. Morningstar categories help investors and investment professionals make meaningful comparisons between funds. The categories make it easier to build well-diversified portfolios, assess potential risk, and identify top-performing funds. We place funds in a given category based on their portfolio statistics and compositions over the past three years. If the fund is new and has no portfolio history, we estimate where it will fall before giving it a more permanent category assignment. When necessary, we may change a category assignment based on recent changes to the portfolio.

Fund Overview

Category	Large Blend
Fund Family	Vanguard
Net Assets	1.4T
YTD Return	14.16%
Yield	1.37%
Morningstar Rating	★★★
Inception Date	May 23, 2001

Fund Operations

Last Dividend	0.73
Last Cap Gain	41.00
Holdings Turnover	3.00%
Average for Category	N/A

Fees & Expenses

Expense		VTSMX	Category Average
Annual Report Expense Ratio (net)		0.03%	0.84%
Prospectus Net Expense Ratio		0.03%	N/A
Prospectus Gross Expense Ratio		0.03%	N/A
Max 12b1 Fee		N/A	N/A
Max Front End Sales Load		N/A	5.18%
Max Deferred Sales Load		N/A	1.28%
3 Yr Expense Projection		0	N/A
5 Yr Expense Projection		0	N/A
10 Yr Expense Projection		0	N/A

Profile:

- **Investment valuation box:** This fund predominantly channels its investments into "Blended-Large Size Companies." While it echoes the trajectory of every US company, its allocation is steered by company market cap sizes. Thus, mammoth companies dictate the majority of the index.

- ○ **Note:** The term "Blended" encapsulates a mix of growth-type stocks (representing companies projected to burgeon at an impressive rate, like Amazon, which, though not currently highly profitable, boasts expansive growth potential) and value-type stocks (representing companies whose stock prices are attractively economical compared to their earnings, such as the relatively steady JPMorgan Chase Bank).

- **Fees & expenses:** Ensure there's no front or back sales load; in this case, there isn't.

- **Performance (as of 8/2023):**

  - ○ Year to date (YTD): 14.16 percent

  - ○ Over three years: 13.0 percent

  - ○ Over ten years: 12.7 percent

Overall Impression:

VTSMX emerges as an attractive, pocket-friendly index fund boasting robust average returns. Vanguard's reputation is anchored in offering both economical and high-performing options.

Example #2: Invesco Oppenheimer Main Street Fund Class A (MSIGX)

Let's dive into MSIGX, another mutual fund you might encounter in your 401(k). While it also tracks all US companies, akin to the Vanguard Total Stock Market Index, a deeper look reveals some concerning costs. Navigate to Yahoo Finance and input the MSIGX ticker for a detailed overview.

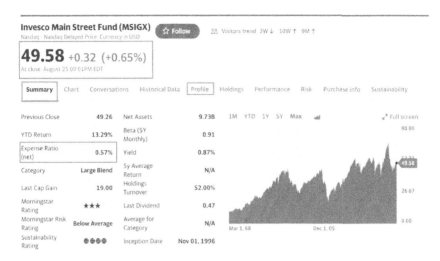

Summary:

- **Current price per share:** $49.58 (Again, this metric isn't important)

- **Expense ratio (cost of fund):** 0.57 percent annually. In comparison to its counterparts, this is relatively expensive.

Invesco Oppenheimer Main Street Fund Class A

AIM Equity Funds (Invesco Equity Funds)
11 Greenway Plaza.Suite 100
Houston, TX 77046
800-959-4246

Management Information

Manind Govil, Lead Manager since May 18, 2009
Mani Govil serves as head of the Main Street Team and lead portfolio manager of Main Street Fund. Mani has more than 15 years of experience managing core equity portfolios and was named one of the "20 Rising Stars" in the mutual fund industry by Institutional Investor in 2008. Prior to joining OppenheimerFunds in May 2009, Mani managed the RS Large Cap Alpha Fund (formerly Guardian Park Avenue Fund) from August 2005 to March 2009. Mani first managed the fund at Guardian Life Insurance Company from August 2005 to October 2006 and then at RS Investments, now a unit of Guardian, from October 2006 to March 2009. At RS, Mani worked as head of core equity investments and lead portfolio manager for large-cap blend/core equity. At Guardian, Mani served as head of equity investments and lead portfolio manager for large-cap blend/core equity. Earlier in his career, as co-head of equities and head of research at Mercantile Capital Advisers, Mani managed the Mercantile Growth and Income Fund. He holds an M.B.A from the University of Cincinnati and a B.Comm. degree from the University of Bombay, India. Mani is a CFA charterholder.

Morningstar Style Box

Yahoo partners with Morningstar a leading market research and investment data group to help investors rate and compare funds on Yahoo Finance. The Morningstar Category is shown next to the Morningstar Style Box which identifies a fund's investment

Fund Overview

Category	Large Blend
Fund Family	Invesco
Net Assets	8.75B
YTD Return	-7.81%
Yield	0.89%
Morningstar Rating	★★★
Inception Date	Feb 2, 1988

Fund Operations

Last Dividend	0.43
Last Cap Gain	0.00
Holdings Turnover	7.00%
Average for Category	N/A

Fees & Expenses

Expense	MSIGX	Category Average
Annual Report Expense Ratio (net)	0.85%	0.94%
Prospectus Net Expense Ratio	0.85%	N/A
Prospectus Gross Expense Ratio	0.85%	N/A
Max 12b1 Fee	0.25%	N/A
Max Front End Sales Load	5.50%	5.27%
Max Deferred Sales Load	N/A	1.38%

Profile:

- **Investment valuation box:** The fund predominantly channels its investments into "Large Size Companies," mirroring the direction we saw with the Vanguard Total Stock Market Index.

    - **Fees & expenses**: There's a glaring front sales load of 5.50 percent. This is a substantial deterrent. To put it in perspective, an investment of $100 immediately incurs a $5.50 charge just to purchase the fund.

- **Performance (for 2022):**

    - Year to date (YTD): 13.29 percent

    - Over five years: 8.93 percent

○ Over ten years: 10.42 percent

Overall Impression:

Regrettably, MSIGX is pretty awful as a broad-market stock fund due to its hidden fees. Its actively managed nature, exorbitant expense ratio, and the audacity to charge an upfront fee of 5.5 percent make it a hard pass. Consequently, even though it tracks a similar index, its post-fee performance lags behind the Vanguard total stock index fund. A prudent investor would steer clear.

(V) The Era of Target Date Retirement Funds and Robo-Advisers: Choosing the Right Brokerage.

What about Target-Date Retirement Funds?

Feeling overwhelmed with all the financial jargon? Thinking, "Dat, I pursued optometry, not finance!"? That's totally fine.

While here at ODs on Finance we advocate the DIY investing approach, we do recognize that investing isn't everyone's cup of tea, especially for busy professionals like doctors. If you're reading this, you're already ahead with a grasp of the essentials.

Want a hassle-free solution? Consider a Target-Date Retirement Mutual Fund. Think of it as the One Ring to rule them all in investing (and, yes, that checks our Lord of the Rings reference for the day). Most 401(k) or retirement plans offer these funds. You simply select a fund that aligns with your projected retirement year.

Financial Tip

Target-date retirement funds simplify investing. They auto-balance between stocks and bonds annually. In your thirties? Expect more stock exposure for higher returns, though with increased risk.

For instance, if you're thirty in 2020 and aiming to retire around 2055, you might opt for the **Vanguard Target Retirement 2050 Fund Investor Shares (VFIFX)**. While its 0.15 percent expense ratio is reasonable, always scrutinize; some funds can levy up to 0.80 percent. And if you fancy a stock-heavy approach, just pick a later target year.

Your choice doesn't set off any alarms in your 401(k), even if the fund date slightly differs from your retirement year. The trade-off? Less control and slightly higher costs than an S&P 500 Index fund.

For novices, these funds are an excellent starting point. As you gain investing prowess, you can diversify.

What about Robo-Advisers?

Despite the futuristic name, they aren't sci-fi robots making stock choices for you. Or are they?

Robo-advisers are online platforms using algorithms to determine your ideal investment mix, considering your risk appetite and time horizon. They also periodically recalibrate your assets. With no humans in the loop, fees are significantly lower, typically between 0.25 percent to 0.50 percent, versus traditional advisers who charge 1–2 percent.

Platforms like Betterment and Wealthfront have resonated

particularly well with millennials. They've gamified investing, offering intuitive interfaces and visual analytics.

Financial Tip

Essentially, robo-advisers mirror the functions of basic low-cost target-date retirement mutual funds but add some bells and whistles. If you're alright with the slight fee hike, dive in!

Which Brokerage Should I Invest With?

A brokerage is an online middleman facilitating trades between investors. Here, you house accounts like retirement plans and taxable accounts. Those with kids might also explore 529 college accounts.

We endorse economical, versatile online brokerages. Here's a snapshot:

- **Vanguard:** Pioneers of discount brokerage, they remain a go-to for passive investors with an array of funds and free index funds/ETF options. Its user interface could be improved.

  - Trading fee: $0

  - Account minimum: 0 percent

- **Fidelity:** A synthesis of $0 commissions, stellar research, and an intuitive app. It boasts a range of funds and two hundred-plus branches for face-to-face consultations.

  - Trading fee: $0

  - Account minimum: 0 percent

- **E-Trade**: Renowned for diverse investments and research support. While they lean toward active traders, they also cater to the long-term crowd with a plethora of free mutual funds/ETFs.

  - Trading fee: $0

  - Account minimum: 0 percent

- **Charles Schwab:** Recently, they've been aggressive in cutting down costs, offering fractional stock shares, and eliminating most fees, making it one of the most affordable options.

  - Trading fee: $0

  - Account minimum: 0 percent

Financial Tip

Caution: Robinhood initially made waves among younger millennials by pioneering zero-commission trading fees. However, this advantage has been diluted, as other major brokerages now offer similar zero-commission structures. Coupled with technical issues in 2020, a restricted stock/ETF/mutual fund selection, subpar tax services, and limited account and service options, Robinhood may not be the ideal choice for the more serious investor.

(VI) Tracking Investment Performance and Other Wealth-Building Insights

How to Monitor Your Investments and Track Performance

The last step of any investing game plan involves monitoring your investments and performance. You don't need to obsessively check it daily; however, it's advisable to review it at least once a month. Setting an investment plan in motion, such as selecting a target date for retirement or a passive stock index fund, is straightforward. Still, it's essential not to neglect it thereafter.

Regularly monitoring your finances can be rewarding, especially when you observe your investments growing and your student debt decreasing each month. Think of every dollar you've invested as hundreds of mini-workers, tirelessly working around the clock to earn you passive income.

Personal Capital (Free Website + Mobile)

This free app allows you to link all your bank, investment brokerage, retirement, and student loan accounts. It consolidates everything into a comprehensive dashboard, displaying your asset allocations, the ratio of stocks to bonds, total fees paid in funds, and overall net worth (don't fret if it's in the negative due to student debt). Additionally, it provides a complimentary retirement planner to guide you on your retirement goals and offers insights about the effectiveness of your financial plan. And, yes, did we mention it's free?

For those who prefer a more traditional approach, a straightforward Microsoft Excel sheet can effectively track your earnings.

Common Questions About Investing

When should I start investing?

Now is the best time to start investing, irrespective of the market's state. Warren Buffet, the legendary investor, owes much of his wealth to beginning his investment journey early— purchasing his first stock at eleven. The power of compounding is most effective over extended periods. So start immediately.

What are the best stock market investments?

Low-cost index funds, such as the S&P 500 Index or Total Stock Market Index, are top contenders. By investing in these funds, you're essentially acquiring a substantial portion of the stock market in one go. This approach ensures you neither outperform or underperform the market. Essentially, you're betting on the US economy. Historically, those who trade individual stocks often lag behind the market over the long haul.

Is stock trading recommended for beginners?

We caution against beginners dabbling in individual stocks. Moreover, we advise against trading stocks, even for seasoned investors. Regularly buying and selling stocks can lead to tax inefficiencies, particularly if your gains (held for less than a year) are taxed as regular income. Such frequent transactions can also induce erratic decision-making, succumbing to the temptation of market timing.

Instead, we champion a buy-and-hold strategy, focusing on low-cost index funds, and advocate dollar-cost averaging— consistently investing a predetermined sum through market highs and lows.

How should I invest money I might need soon? And is a conservative approach advisable?

Investing boils down to two primary considerations:

- **Time horizon:** When will you need the money?
- **Risk tolerance**: How much risk are you comfortable with?

First, let's delve into the time horizon. If your investment goals stretch into the distant future, like retirement, it's wise to allocate a significant portion of your investment to stocks, approaching 90 percent. This strategy will likely help your funds grow and stay ahead of inflation. However, as you edge closer to your goal, consider shifting your focus, reducing stock allocation, and incorporating more bonds.

On the other hand, if your investment horizon is relatively short (under five years)—say, for a down payment on a house—it might not be advisable to invest in stocks.

For more insights on this, refer to: The OD's Guide to Short-Term Investing.

Next, let's discuss risk tolerance, which is highly individualized and not strictly age dependent.

To provide some perspective, I view myself as an aggressive investor, maintaining a portfolio that's 100 percent stocks.

What's the rationale behind this?

- I'm currently in my thirties, which means I'm looking at an investment horizon that spans over thirty years.

- When I graduated back in 2015, at twenty-eight, I had no savings to speak of and was burdened with student debt exceeding $230k. As a result, playing it "safe" with a higher bond allocation doesn't seem feasible for me.

- Mentally, I've braced myself for market fluctuations. A case in point is the 2020 Coronavirus Crisis, which saw the S&P 500 Index plummet nearly 28 percent. While the sea of red numbers was unnerving, I resisted the urge to sell. This episode was a testament to my resilience as an investor. Ultimately, the best investment strategy is one that lets you sleep soundly at night.

It's crucial to remember that the stock market has its highs and lows. If you find yourself easily spooked by these fluctuations, a more conservative approach, with a pronounced bond allocation, might be more your speed.

Summary

Kudos for reaching the conclusion of this comprehensive guide! Inhale deeply. You've now mastered the basics of Investing 101. Quite simple when juxtaposed with learning intricate neural pathways, right?

By grasping these rudiments, you're poised to be a genuine contender in the stock market.

Our intent behind this guide was twofold:

- **(1) Render the content engaging and straightforward.**

- **(2) Highlight potential pitfalls, especially for students and young doctors.**

Investing demands patience, consistent effort, and resilience, rather than financial wizardry. Often, young doctors, eager for quick success, can be lured into dubious ventures.

Many doctors falter financially because they either overlook the significance of financial literacy or exhibit overconfidence. This oversight, combined with a lack of structured education on personal finance and investment, is a recipe for disaster.

Many financial representatives, disguised as advisors, might exploit doctors' trusting demeanor. Remember, financial advisors aren't bound by an oath to prioritize your interests. Even "fiduciary-certified" advisors can exhibit biases, albeit unconsciously. **Your strongest defense?** Educate yourself and approach every piece of advice with discernment.

Financial Tip

Many doctors falter financially due to their hectic schedules or overconfidence in their financial prowess. This gap in financial knowledge, coupled with the absence of structured education on personal finance, renders them vulnerable to unscrupulous financial advisers or insurance salespeople.

Always be inquisitive, scrutinizing every piece of information, ensuring it aligns with your goals. As with all things, trust but verify.

Key Takeaways:

- Understanding the basics of investing and familiarizing yourself with financial terminology are fundamental to your financial literacy. Such knowledge will pave the way for future wealth, even if you eventually choose to have a professional manage your finances.

- A broad market Low-Cost & Passive Stock Index Fund (ETF) often emerges as the optimal choice for doctors due to its attributes: low fees, outstanding performance, tax efficiency, tax-saving benefits, and risk minimization.

- Often, a straightforward three-fund portfolio can outshine more complex strategies. Complexity does not always guarantee superior performance.

- A widely accepted principle for long-term investing is this: as you approach retirement, gradually tilt your portfolio in favor of bonds. It's wise to avoid placing funds you'll need within the next three to five years in the stock market, given the potential for market downturns.

- Rebalancing your portfolio essentially entails adjusting it to maintain your desired stock-to-bond ratio. It's recommended to keep this process straightforward, and an annual rebalancing is typically sufficient.

- Buying individual stocks isn't a mandatory step for investment success. For the majority, we champion low-cost, passive stock index funds as the primary component of their portfolios. Stay committed to this approach, and you're likely to see positive outcomes.

- Be vigilant about funds with high expense ratios, as these fees can significantly erode your portfolio's returns.

- Target-date retirement funds offer a streamlined investing experience and are ideal for those who prefer a hands-off approach. These funds automatically adjust the stock-to-bond ratio annually, becoming more conservative as you near retirement.

- Always bear in mind that while the stock market will experience ups and downs, it has historically trended upward over extended periods. Resist the urge to time the market! The duration you remain invested in the market is often a reliable indicator of financial success.

CHAPTER 13:

PLANNING FOR RETIREMENT | BY DAT BUI, OD

> As far as your personal goals are and what you
> actually want to do with your life, it should never
> have to do with the government. You should never
> depend on the government for your retirement,
> your financial security, for anything. If you do,
> you're screwed.
> —**Drew Carey**

There's a poignant story about an optometrist that I'd like to share, one that profoundly impacted my financial journey. During my early days as a new doctor, I worked a fill-in shift at LensCrafter in the Bay Area, California. There, I met Alan, a kindly older Asian gentleman in his mid-eighties. Alan and I shared duties that day, working in tandem across different shifts in various offices around the area. His care for his patients was evident, but his age made physical movement visibly difficult.

Eventually, I asked, *"Alan, I hope this isn't intrusive, but why are you still working at this age?"* His pause spoke volumes, and he confided: *"Dat, early in my career, I lived lavishly in San Francisco, enjoying the perks of my salary. My luxurious apartment, frequent travels, and lifestyle choices meant I rarely saved. As years rolled by, debts mounted, from mortgages to medical bills. A divorce and my children's ongoing college expenses further strained my finances. I'd have loved to retire earlier, but I couldn't."*

Leaning in, he earnestly added, *"Dat, time is a gift when you're young. Prepare for retirement. Learn from my mistakes."*

That night, my shelves were filled with all the personal finance books I could buy. Alan's words became my guiding principle, underscoring the importance of retirement planning, especially for budding professionals like us.

While boards and exams might occupy your mind now as an optometry student, soon you'll be drawing a sizable paycheck. After eight-plus years of rigorous studies, the allure of a lavish life will beckon. The "YOLO" mindset might seem appealing now (though this slang might be passé by 2023!), but remember: just as you meticulously plan your academic career, retirement planning is crucial.

Many misconstrue retirement as a never-ending vacation. In truth, it's about achieving financial freedom—the liberty to pursue passions, donate, travel, or continue working without monetary constraints.

That is the true goal of retirement.

However, with our limited monthly cash flows and myriad of expenses, setting aside funds for a distant retirement can be challenging.

Before delving into retirement strategies, consider these four essential financial milestones:

- **Goal 1: Understand and budget your expenses.**
- **Goal 2: Establish a three-to-six-month emergency fund.**
- **Goal 3: Maximize employer matches in retirement funds.**
- **Goal 4: Eliminate high-interest debts.**

Goal 1: Understand Your Expenses and How to Budget

In chapter 6, we delved into the importance of living frugally, akin to a struggling student, and the significance of budgeting. If you need to refresh your memory, I urge you to revisit that chapter. To put it plainly, you won't have a clear idea of how much you can allocate toward retirement, settling your student loans, or other financial goals if you're unaware of your residual income at the end of the month.

Here Are the Five Steps for Starting a Budget

- **(1) List ALL monthly income:** This includes W2, 1099 fill-in, side business income, and any other income sources. Document them at the onset of each month.

  - Note: For irregular income streams, such as the influx of income optometrists might experience during the holiday season, compute a monthly average as an estimate.

- **(2) List ALL fixed monthly expenses:** These can include rent, house mortgage/property tax, utilities, car insurance, student loan payments, other consumer debt (like credit card or car lease) minimum payments, health/disability insurance, and the minimum contribution toward retirement.

  - Note: An ideal contribution to your retirement IRA/401(k) would be at least 10 percent of your total gross income while you're still clearing student debt, and preferably 20 percent once all debts are squared away.

- **(3) Outline your essential monthly needs:** Common examples are groceries, vehicular expenses like gas and parking, or even public transportation costs and basic household necessities.

- **(4) Specify your monthly desires:** Think of expenses related to dining out, fast food, entertainment avenues like Netflix or Spotify, your daily coffee runs, outings to bars, mobile phone bills, personal grooming, and hygiene, among others.

- **(5) Tally your monthly income and expenses:** If your calculations reveal your income surpassing your expenditures, you're on the right track. Utilize the surplus to address other financial aspirations.

It does seem straightforward, doesn't it? Then, one might wonder, why do countless individuals struggle with adhering to their budget? The core issue is societal; we often blur the lines between our needs and desires. The thought processes like, "I absolutely must keep my Netflix subscription," or, "I can't possibly start my day without my $5 Starbucks Frappuccino," divert our attention from genuine necessities vital for a comfortable life.

This budgeting exercise is designed to help you discern what truly counts. For the initial month, adopt a more adaptable approach to each category. This allows for adjustments in the allocated amounts in the subsequent months. Generally, it's around the third month that most people find their budget stabilizing. So a touch of initial hiccups shouldn't deter you.

Make it a habit to assess your budget on a monthly basis. Reflect on the past month to identify areas where you stayed on track and where you might've overshot. Based on this, recalibrate as necessary. And a word of advice—it's unwise to arbitrarily bump up your entertainment budget by a significant amount, say $500, just because an event like Coachella is on the horizon.

Goal 2: Building an Emergency Fund (Three to Six Months of Expenses)

Ever found yourself pondering, "What if my car transmission gives out? What if I fracture my arm and I'm relegated to conducting eye exams with one hand? What if I'm unexpectedly unemployed and struggle to secure another job?"

Such what-if scenarios can materialize unpredictably, jeopardizing our financial stability and, in the worst cases, thrusting many into debilitating debt or, even graver, bankruptcy.

Enter the pivotal role of a robust emergency fund. Think of it as your financial cushion or an "Oh CRAP" reserve, ensuring peace of mind. It arms you against life's unforeseen financial storms. Though we, as doctors, often lean toward precision in our actions and expectations, life seldom operates with the same predictability, and unforeseen circumstances can potentially cripple us financially.

On a brighter note, optometrists tend to enjoy commendable job security. When in need, many find solace in sporadic fill-in shifts at various offices to offset expenses, or even contemplate relocating to less populated regions where their earning potential often multiplies.

A standard recommendation is to amass funds equivalent to a minimum of three months' worth of expenses (not income). Some might need less, especially if they have family nearby ready to lend financial support in tight spots.

Now, you might be pondering—**"Could I utilize my credit card for emergencies?"**

The answer is a resounding NO! Relying on credit cards for emergencies can lead individuals down the treacherous path of overwhelming debt. Be wiser than the masses.

So what qualifies as a genuine emergency?

Many tend to blur these lines. A tempting 50-percent-off sale at Nordstrom does NOT constitute an emergency. Neither does the allure of the latest iPhone or a brand-new car. Genuine emergencies are those unforeseen events that, if not planned for, can wreak havoc on your finances.

As you cultivate financial acumen and refine your budgeting skills, you'll likely encounter fewer financial emergencies.

Where Should You Store Your Emergency Fund?

It should be stashed in a secure (FDIC-insured), liquid (readily accessible) place, preferably where it can accrue some interest. Typically, an online high-yield savings account fits the bill or even your standard checking account.

Goal 3: Maximize Contributions to Primary Retirement Funds (401(k), SEP/SIMPLE IRA) Matching Employer's Contribution

If your employment offers retirement benefits like a 401(k) and there's an employer matching scheme (commonly up to 6 percent), ensure you contribute to claim that match fully. It's akin to free money and represents a valuable chunk of your compensation.

To illustrate, a prevalent employer match might be 50 percent of your contribution up to 6 percent of your annual earnings. While it may sound intricate, it essentially translates to an additional 3 percent of your yearly salary.

Goal 4: Clear High-Interest Debt (Above 8 Percent) Such as Credit Card Balances and Car Lease Loans

This is paramount. The logic is straightforward: if you're grappling with a high-interest debt, say between 8–12 percent on a credit card, prioritize clearing this debt without delay. You'll curtail more in interest expenses this way than what you might earn from a 10 percent return in stock investments, especially after accounting for taxes on such gains. Plus, eliminating these high-interest debts promises a guaranteed return, devoid of the uncertainties that investments inherently possess.

How Much Do I Need for Retirement?

As you draft a game plan for your financial goals, let's delve deeper into mastering retirement planning.

Think of a retirement sum: $50,000? $100,000? $750,000? Chances are, you might be far from accurate. A widely accepted guideline suggests:

> **25 × Post-Retirement Expenses = Total Amount Needed in Retirement Funds**

This rule of thumb is based on the following:

- An average market return of 7 percent

- A retirement age of sixty-five, assuming thirty more years of life

- No outstanding debts, like credit cards, mortgages, or student loans, by retirement

- Excluding Social Security benefits, approximated at $42,651 annually as of 2023, given the unpredictable nature of government tax policies

- No additional income from side businesses

- Abiding by a safe 4 percent withdrawal rate

- Adjustments for inflation

What's the 4% Rule?

The Trinity study proposes that retirees can withdraw 4 percent of their funds annually without a significant reduction in the principal amount. This accounts for a 3 percent inflation, coupled with a 7 percent market gain.

Example

Dr. Retina, sixty-five, plans to retire. He's debt-free and owns his home. Due to aging, his health insurance costs have surged. To maintain his lifestyle and cater to yearly expenses, including some leisure activities, he needs $80,000 annually. Using the 25x rule, he'd require around $2 million in retirement savings.

Surprisingly, the average 401(k) balance for Americans sixty-five and older is just $192,877. If you adhere to the 4 percent rule, this translates to a meager $7,715 yearly or less than $650 monthly, significantly well below the national poverty level.

Over thirty-five years, assuming a 7 percent market gain, it suggests that the average American only sets aside around $105 per month for retirement.

Achieving a $2 million retirement fund might seem daunting. But remember, time coupled with the magic of compounding interest, tax breaks, and a steady salary can boost your retirement returns.

The Power of Compounding Interest

You have probably heard this term many times before! Basically, if you simply put a small amount away today and let it stay there for thirty years, then it will exponentially grow each year.

	Smart Investor	Late Investor	Hard Investor
20			
25	14,369.15		
30	34,759.27		
35	49,324.10	14,369.15	14,369.15
40	69,991.88	34,759.27	34,759.27
45	99,319.87	49,324.10	63,693.25
50	140,936.87	69,991.88	104,751.14
55	199,992.23	99,319.87	163,013.10
60	283,792.96	140,936.87	245,688.00
65	402,707.86	199,992.23	363,005.32

Example: Let's look at three different doctor investors in this example. Doctor A is a *smart investor,* Doctor B is the *late investor,* and Doctor C is the *hard investor.* Let's assume a typical **7 percent interest market rate,** where the shaded dark area indicates the years in which $200 a month was saved.

SMART INVESTOR	LATE INVESTOR	HARD INVESTOR
Age 25 to 35: $200/Month	Age 35 to 45: $200/Month	Age 35 to 65: $200/Month

TOTAL INVESTING: **10YRS**	TOTAL INVESTING: **10YRS**	TOTAL INVESTING: **30YRS**
RETIREMENT= $402,707	RETIREMENT= $199,992	RETIREMENT= $363,005

The Smart Investor has **DOUBLE** the amount compared to the Late Investor by investing 10 years earlier ($402,707 vs $199,992).

The Hard Investor still has **$39,702.54** *less* than Smart Investor, despite investing **MORE money** and for **20+ year longer** ($363,005 vs $402,707).

- **Doctor A, smart investor**, starts saving $200 per month at age twenty-five until he is thirty-five years old, then stops all contributions. He invests for a total of ten years.

- **Doctor B, late investor**, starts saving $200 per month at age thirty-five until he is forty-five years old, then stops all contributions. He invests for a total of ten years.

- **Doctor C, hard investor**, starts saving at $200 per month at age thirty-five until he retires at sixty-five (typical retirement age). He invests for a duration of thirty years while contributing the most money over his lifetime.

At the time of retirement age, which is sixty-five years old for all three investors, we can see a few surprising results:

- By simply investing earlier at age twenty-five (ten years before the late investor), the **smart investor has <u>DOUBLE</u> the amount compared to the late investor** ($402,707 compared to $199,992).

- The hard investor started saving at age thirty-five (ten years behind the smart investor), and even though he tries to catch up and save an extra $200 per month until he retires at sixty-five, the **hard investor still has $39,702.54 less than the smart investor** ($363,005 vs. $402,707).

- In addition, the hard investor put in **more time and thus more** money contributions compared to the shorter investing time by the smart investor (thirty years vs. ten years).

The moral of the story? The sooner you start saving, the quicker you will see the power of compound interest.

What Is the Latte Factor?

The *latte factor* is a renowned theory spotlighting the power of compounding even on modest daily expenses. Take, for instance, a $4 latte. Multiply that by 365 days, and you spend a considerable $1,460 annually. Imagine investing this sum every year from age thirty to sixty-five, with a conservative annual market return of 7 percent. By age sixty-five, that habitual cup of coffee would amount to a staggering $214,770.

A quick note: This isn't a jab at coffee lovers. Rather, it underscores how seemingly trivial expenses accumulate over time. Prioritizing your finances—like maintaining a healthy saving rate and wise investments—ensures you can occasionally indulge in life's small pleasures without jeopardizing your future.

What about Social Security?

I hate to burst your bubble, but the future of the Social Security program remains uncertain. By 2033, it's projected that the government will be capable of disbursing only 77 percent of the promised benefits to current Social Security recipients. This indicates that younger generations may receive significantly smaller monthly payouts compared to the older baby boomer cohort.

Given the strides in healthcare, people today are outliving the average life expectancies—seventy-six for males and eighty-one for females. Frankly, the government isn't equipped for this longevity.

Furthermore, even if we optimistically assume that Social Security benefits will be fully honored, the payout may not be as substantial as hoped. Consider a typical optometrist with an average annual salary of $120,000. **As of 2023, they could anticipate a monthly retirement benefit check of approximately $3,554. Annually, that's a mere $42,651**—far below the US poverty threshold and certainly not inflation-proof for their retirement years.

In essence, it's unwise to solely bank on Social Security for your retirement. If you do end up receiving some benefits—fantastic! Think of it as a delightful bonus.

Curious about your retirement trajectory? Explore our ONLINE RETIREMENT CALCULATOR.

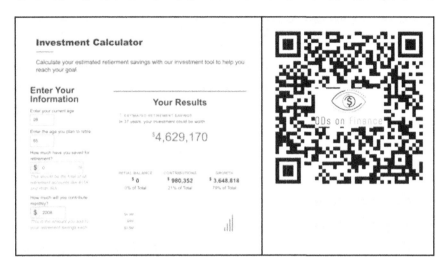

Which Retirement Accounts Are Right for You?

Just hang on tight because I know this is going to sound kind of dry and boring as an optometry student. But we're here to guide you through the retirement options best suited to your situation, ensuring you maximize your tax savings by choosing the right accounts.

> (1) 8 Types of Retirement Accounts
>
> (2) Roth vs. Traditional: 6 Reasons to Consider a Roth 401(k)
>
> (3) Understanding Roth IRA and the Backdoor Roth IRA
>
> (4) The Lowdown on the Health Savings Account (HSA)
>
> (5) Six Doctor Retirement Examples

Now, let's quickly break down the various retirement plans available. Once we've covered the basics, we'll delve into determining the perfect fit for your financial landscape.

8 Basics Types of Retirement Plans Offered (2023)

Employer-Provided 401K/403B/457B

Who?
Company-provided account for Employees

Contributions
Can contribute **Pre-Tax Deductible dollar** up to **$22,500** (Extra $7,500 catch-up for > Age 50. Employer automatically deduct pre-tax contributions on your paycheck.

Taxes
All withdrawals are taxed at income rate after age 55, but additional 10% Penalty imposed if withdrawal made before retirement age 55

Pros:

- Roth option may be available depending on your employer
- Usually have an employer match (1-10%)
- Able to borrow money as 5-year loan (limited to 50% of 401K fund or $50,000, whichever is less)
- Able to withdraw without penalty due to hardship such as disability and high medical expense

Cons:

- Funds selection may be great or very poor. Fund cost can vary in price or have high administration yearly fees depending on company
- Must leave previous company to roll-over to another 401K with new employer or roll-over into personal IRA

Solo/Individual 401K

Who?
Self-employed 1099 individual or Business owner with no employees (other than spouse)

Contributions
Can contribute **Pre-Tax Deductible dollars - $22,500,** toward the employee/employer's 401K, along with an employer's match/contribution (profit-sharing) up **$66,000 Total (or Max 100% of total income)**, whichever is less.

Taxes
All withdrawals are taxed at income rate after age 55 but additional 10% Penalty imposed if withdrawal made before retirement age

Pros:
o Able to borrow money as 5-year loan (limited to only 50% of 401K or $50,000, whichever is less).
o Able to withdraw without penalty due to hardship such as disability and high medical expense

Cons:
o Harder to set up and require a plan administer like Vanguard

Traditional Individual Retirement Account (Trad-IRA)

Who?
Any earned-income individual (W2 or 1099)

Contributions
Can contribute up to **$6,500 Pre-tax Deductible dollars (**Extra $1,000 catch-up for >Age 50). Will have **Modified Adjusted Gross income (MAGI)** limit if Optometrist already have a **main employer retirement plan like 401K or SIMPLE IRA**

Single: Max MAGI income= $83,000 (start to phase out contribution level at $73,000)

Married filing jointly: Max MAGI income = $136,000 (start to phase out contribution level at $116,000)

Taxes
All withdrawals are taxed at income rate after 59 ½ but additional 10% Penalty imposed if withdrawal made prior to retirement age

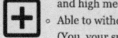

Pros:
- Easy to set up with great fund choices
- Able to withdraw without penalty due to hardship such as disability and high medical expense
- Able to withdraw without penalty for qualified Higher education (You, your spouse or your children or grandchildren)
- Able to withdraw without penalty up to $10,000 per spouse for 1st home purchase (You, spouse, grandparents or children/grandchildren)

Cons:
- Low contribution Limit
- Most ODs' income will be too high or they will already have a main Employer retirement account

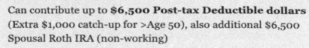

Roth Individual Retirement Account (Roth-IRA)

Who?

Any earned-income individual (W2 or 1099)

Contributions

Can contribute up to **$6,500 Post-tax Deductible dollars** (Extra $1,000 catch-up for >Age 50), also additional $6,500 Spousal Roth IRA (non-working)

<u>Single:</u> Max MAGI income= $153,000 (start to phase out contribution level at $138,000)

<u>Married filing jointly:</u> Max MAGI income = $228,000 (start to phase out contribution level at $218,000)

Taxes

Contributions (what you put in) can be withdrawn at any time, without taxes or penalty. If you withdraw earnings (a.k.a. gains) before age 59 ½ then they will be taxed as income tax rate +10% penalty. Otherwise, withdrawal on gains will be tax-free after 59 ½

Pros:

- Easy to set up with great fund choices
- Tax-free Growth
- Able to withdraw CONTRIBUTIONS Anytime (since it is funded with post-tax already) with tax or 10% Penalty PRIOR TO 59 1/2
- Able to withdraw EARNING without penalty due to hardship such as disability and high medical expense **(After 5 years)**
- Able to withdraw EARNING without penalty for qualified Higher education like for you, your spouse or your children or grandchildren **(After 5 years)**
- Able to withdraw EARNING without penalty up to $10,000 per spouse for 1st home purchase for you, spouse, grandparents or children/grandchildren) **(After 5 years)**

Cons:

- Low contribution Limit
- Max Income limit, but able to do **Backdoor Roth IRA**
- **5 years Withdrawal Rule:**The first Roth IRA five-year rule is used to determine if the earnings (interest) from your Roth IRA are tax-free. To be tax-free, you must withdraw the earnings: *(1) On or after the date you turn 59 (2) At least five tax years after the first contribution to any Roth IRA you own*

Saving Incentive Match Plan IRA (SIMPLE-IRA)

Who?
Business with <100 employees or self-employed individuals

Contributions
Can contribute **Pre-Tax Deductible Dollars** up to **$15,500** (Extra $3,500 catch-up for > Age 50))

Taxes
All withdrawals are taxed at income rate after 59 ½ but Additional 10% Penalty imposed if withdrawal made prior to retirement age

Pros:

- Easier and more affordable to set for small business
- Able to withdraw without penalty due to hardship such as disability and high medical expense
- Able to withdraw without penalty for qualified Higher education (You, your spouse or your children or grandchildren)
- Able to withdraw without penalty up to $10,000 per spouse for 1st home purchase (You, spouse, grandparents or children/grandchildren)

Cons:

- Lower contribution Limit
- No Roth Option
- Cannot do Backdoor Roth IRA due to pro-rata rule if above MAGI income limits

Self-Employed IRA (SEP-IRA)

Who?

Self-employed 1099 individual or small business owner (including those with employees

Contributions

Pre-Tax Deductible **dollar for 1099 income. Can contribute up to $66,000 (max is 25% of net income).** You simply claim the deduction when you file taxes on your 1099 income or via employer paycheck.

Employer of SEP IRA can offer it to their employees and thus automatically deduct pre-tax contributions on your paycheck or you can deduct it during tax filing.

Taxes

All withdrawals are taxed at income rate after 59 ½, but Additional 10% Penalty imposed if withdrawal made prior to retirement age

Pros:

- Easy to set up with great fund choices
- Able to withdraw without penalty due to hardship such as disability and high medical expense
- Able to withdraw without penalty for qualified Higher education (You, your spouse or your children or grandchildren)
- Able to withdraw without penalty up to $10,000 per spouse for 1st home purchase (You, spouse, grandparents or children/grandchildren)

Cons:

- No Roth Option
- Cannot do Backdoor Roth IRA due to pro-rata rule if above MAGI income limits

401K with Profit-Sharing Plan (PSP)

Who?

Employer-provided 401K along with a Profit Sharing feature where the employer can make a profit-sharing contribution to employees.

Example: Group of doctor partners

Contributions

Can contribute **Pre-Tax Deductible dollar $22,500** toward the employee/employer's 401K, along with an employer's match/contribution **up to $43,500 match**, but **$66,000 Total (or Max 100% of total income),** whichever is less

Taxes

All withdrawals are taxed at income rate after age 55, but additional 10% penalty imposed if withdrawal made before retirement age

Pros:

o Significant higher Benefits and higher contribution in short period of time, leading to subsidized early retirement

Cons:

o Extremely expensive and overly Complicated.
o Need an administer and cannot discriminate toward higher-paying participants

Defined Benefit Plan (DBP)

Who?

- Small Business with no employees other than the owners and spouses.
- Basically employer-sponsored that pays out monthly benefits upon retirement based in a set formula

Contributions

Employers can only contribute **Pre-Tax Deductible dollars up to $265,000 (or max 100% of average income for 3 highest constructive years)**

Taxes

All withdrawals are taxed at income rate after age 59 ½ but additional 10% Penalty imposed if withdrawal made before retirement age

Upon retirement, can be paid out in 3 ways such as (1) Single life annuity (Fixed monthly benefit until you die, but no further payment to your family survivors upon death), (2) Qualified joint/survivor annuity (your surviving spouse will get benefits until his or her death) or (3) Lump-sum payment.

Pros:

- Significant higher Benefits and higher contribution in short period of time, leading to subsidized early retirement

Cons:

- Extremely expensive and complicated to set up
- Need an administer to prevent an Excise Tax if minimum contribution requirement is not satisfied

Now that you've gotten a quick overview of all the common retirement accounts available to ODs, let's continue with some key concepts. *Feel free to refer back to this chart as a reference.*

What Is the Difference Between Roth vs. Traditional?

Now that we have a broad understanding of the different retirement plans, let's talk about the differences between Roth and Traditional that can apply to either a 401(k) or IRA. This is basically how the government can tax our retirement accounts by forcing you to pay money in taxes now (pre-tax) and later on (post-tax). **Either way, the house, aka the IRS, will get its cut. This can get complicated, so just breathe and read carefully.**

Simply put, with a **traditional 401(k) or traditional IRA**, retirement contributions are made with **PRE-TAX INCOME**, so you pay taxes later in retirement when you withdraw the money. You are taxed depending on your post-retirement income bracket, which should be fairly low since you are not working anymore (usually 12 percent). This is often ideal for most high-earning doctors because we want to **REDUCE OUR TAXABLE INCOME** during our peak career.

In a **Roth 401(k) or Roth-IRA**, retirement contributions are made with **AFTER-TAX INCOME** since you already pay taxes on your income when you get your paycheck (usually W2) so this allows the profit gains to **GROW TAX-FREE** (which is freaking awesome). This is often ideal for low-earning jobs or optometrists during residency. This is also good for the "super-saver" optometrist planning to have a large retirement nest egg!

Example

Let's use a main employer-sponsored 401(k) account (which has a max employee contribution of $22,500 for 2023). For example, Dr. Ptosis has an annual salary of $115,000 with an employer-sponsored 401(k) account and has the choice to go the traditional or Roth route. Which one does he choose?

Since Dr. Ptosis is in a significantly high tax bracket now (Federal = 24 percent), he wants as much deduction as possible to lower his taxable income. So he would want to do traditional 401(k) and contribute pre-tax dollars now. This will allow him to pay the taxes later, when he retires. Assuming that when he retires at sixty-five years old he only has to withdraw less than $40,000 from his retirement accounts for living expenses, essentially, he will only be taxed at 12 percent (one of the lowest tax brackets)! This is the MOST tax-effective way for high-earning doctors.

Financial Tip: Trad 401(k) vs Roth 401(k)

For low earners like optometry residents or students, a Roth 401(k) or Roth IRA is the best route because income will eventually go up in the future, so it is much better to take advantage of their low tax bracket now. While the typical high-earner doctors should look for the tax deduction, thus traditional 401(k) is often the route (assuming they have a modest retirement nest egg of ~$2M and are only taking out $80K for living expenses), when in doubt, the tie always goes to Roth.

6 Reasons Why You Should Consider a Roth-401(k) (EXCEPTION)

Several members of ODs on Finance can be categorized as what I term **"SUPER SAVERS,"** or aggressive investors with a high savings rate (50 percent or more). Many of them are entrepreneurs who anticipate substantial side income during retirement, thereby leading to a sizable retirement nest egg. If one or more of the following scenarios resonate with you, a Roth 401(k) might be a good fit:

(1) Maxing Out Contributions

If you're contributing the maximum allowable amount to both your 401(k) ($22.5K) and Roth IRA ($6.5K) annually, the math adds up quickly. With an assumed 7 percent return from ages twenty-eight to sixty-five, your nest egg could amount to roughly $5M within your retirement accounts. Based on a conservative 4 percent withdrawal rate, this results in annual living expenses of $202,600, placing you in a higher tax bracket.

(2) Entrepreneurial Ventures

Entrepreneurs often have side businesses or rental properties. These ventures could continue generating passive income during retirement, independent of your optometry salary, which could fill your tax brackets.

(3) High Savings Rate

For those who manage to save over 50 percent of their income and live well below their means, the potential is even higher. Even with an annual income of $150K, investing $50,000–75,000 annually at an assumed 7 percent return could result in a nest egg of approximately $8.7M.

A 4 percent withdrawal from this would be around $348,000 annually, possibly pushing you into the highest tax bracket.

(4) Aggressive Investment Strategy

Some investors lean heavily toward growth stocks, especially in tech, rather than diversifying with bonds, even as retirement approaches. While they're conscious of the heightened risks and can stomach significant market volatility, their potential for higher returns might be greater.

(5) Required Minimum Distributions (RMD) at Age 72-75

From age 72-75, the IRS mandates a specified percentage withdrawal from all non-Roth accounts, such as SIMPLE IRAs and traditional 401(k) s. Although several factors can influence the required amount, an average withdrawal rate is typically 3.5 percent. Failure to comply results in a stiff IRS penalty—50 percent of the amount that should've been withdrawn. For instance, with a sizable traditional 401(k) account of $4M, you'd be obligated to withdraw roughly $208K each year, effectively placing you in a higher tax bracket.

(6) Anticipation of Higher Tax Rates

The only certainties in life may be death and taxes. If you predict that due to various factors—government policies, increased spending, or high inflation—tax rates will be steeper by the time you retire (a plausible scenario), then Roth might be the better choice.

In summary, while traditional accounts have their merits, there are unique situations where a Roth 401(k) might be more advantageous. Evaluate your financial landscape and future projections to make an informed choice.

Why Is the Roth IRA so Awesome?

Let's delve into the remarkable attributes of the Roth IRA, a stellar tax-efficient retirement account. Its intricacies are so vast that entire books have been dedicated solely to it. Here, we'll provide a snapshot of why the Roth IRA is such a gem and why it merits inclusion in every high-earner's portfolio. Anyone, even a student, with earned income like a work-study gig, be it from 1099 or W2, can open a Roth IRA through platforms like Vanguard or Fidelity.

For 2023, there's a contribution limit of $6,500, and if you have a non-working spouse, you can contribute an additional $6,500 on their behalf. What's awesome about Roth IRAs is the wide array of cost-effective mutual funds available for investment, granting you more freedom than the default selections in your employer-sponsored 401(k). Plus, opening a Roth IRA is a breeze!

The key feature of a Roth IRA is that contributions are made with after-tax dollars. Hence, these contributions are forever sheltered from taxation. (You've already settled that bill with Uncle Sam!) Moreover, the capital gains, which reflect the growth of your investments, are also tax-exempt upon withdrawal. This dual tax exemption—from both regular income and capital gains tax—distinguishes the Roth IRA from traditional 401(k) s and standard taxable brokerage accounts.

Example

Dr. McLovin, a rather laid-back thirty-year-old in terms of retirement investments, channels just $6,500 annually from his sizable salary into his Roth IRA. Assuming an annual growth rate of 8 percent and a retirement age of sixty-five,

---

his direct contributions will total $227,000.

However, his investment growth would be an impressive $1,013,771!

By merely contributing the minimum, Dr. McLovin is set to retire with a **net worth of $1.2M** (easy path to riches, right?). And the best part? Thanks to the magic of the Roth IRA, the entire $1.2M remains untouched by Uncle Sam.

Had this been stashed in a Traditional 401(k), Dr. McLovin would face taxes on both the contributions and the growth. Assuming he would be in the 15 percent tax bracket during retirement and would withdraw the amount over an extended period, he'd end up forfeiting approximately $180,000 from his $1.2M to taxes.

Withdrawals on Contribution or Gains in a Roth IRA: What You Need to Know

You can access your Roth IRA contributions anytime without incurring taxes or penalties. However, when it comes to withdrawing your gains, the rules are more stringent.

The 5-Year Rule

Gains from your Roth IRA can only be accessed without penalties five years after you've opened the account. For instance, if you contribute to a Roth IRA in February 2020 and assign it for the 2019 tax year (keeping in mind you have until the April 2020 tax deadline to make this Roth contribution for 2019), you'll need to wait until 1/1/2024 to

> touch any earnings from the Roth IRA.

Also, like other retirement accounts, you need to be at least 59 ½ years old to pull out any gains without facing a 10 percent penalty.

What Are Some Exceptions to Avoid the 10 Percent Penalty for Gain Withdrawal?

- **(1) During financial hardships such as disability or exorbitant medical expenses.**

- **(2) Funding higher education** (this can be for you, your spouse, or even children/grandchildren).

- **(3) Up to $10,000 per spouse can be used toward a first-time home purchase** (This also applies to your grandparents or children/grandchildren if it's their inaugural home purchase.)

Many doctors aspire to retire as early as fifty. However, they can't access funds from their traditional 401(k) or IRAs until they're 59 ½. One tactic is to withdraw tax-free Roth IRA CONTRIBUTIONS (not gains) to fund their early retirement and steer clear of the 10 percent penalty. After reaching 59 ½, they can then draw from their traditional 401(k).

Although it's not advisable since Roth IRA funds should primarily be reserved for retirement, some individuals resort to their Roth IRA in extreme financial emergencies, such as life-saving medical procedures.

The Backdoor Roth IRA

You might wonder, "*Most doctors earn well above the $137,000 income threshold, so how can they qualify for a Roth IRA?*"

Good observation!

In 2023, to be eligible for a Roth IRA, single individuals must have a modified adjusted gross income under $153,000 (with phase-out starting at $138,000). For those married and filing jointly, the threshold is $228,000 (with phase-out beginning at $218,000). So how do high-earning professionals manage?

Enter the IRS-permitted loophole: the BACKDOOR Roth IRA.

It's designed for high earners who exceed the Roth IRA MAGI limits but still wish to open a Roth IRA. There are many guides available online detailing the process. In essence, you open a traditional IRA (e.g., through Vanguard), deposit the full $6,000 maximum, and then promptly convert it to a Roth IRA. This can be done annually.

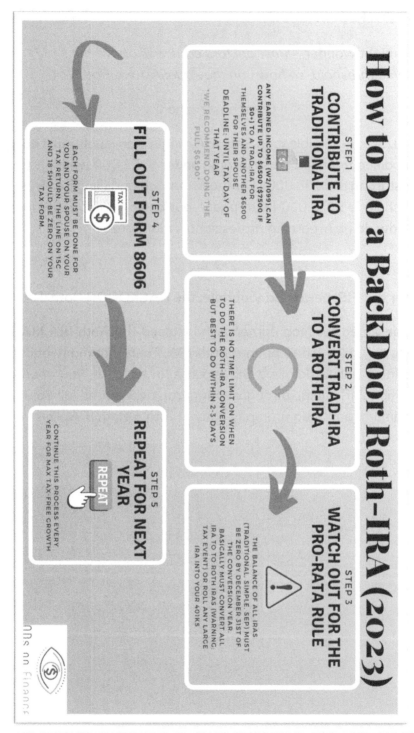

How to Do a BackDoor Roth-IRA (2023)

STEP 1
CONTRIBUTE TO TRADITIONAL IRA

ANY EARNED INCOME (W2/1099) CAN CONTRIBUTE UP TO $6500 ($7500 IF 50+) TO A TRAD-IRA FOR THEMSELVES AND ANOTHER $6500 FOR THEIR SPOUSE

DEADLINE: UNTIL TAX DAY OF THAT YEAR

"WE RECOMMEND DOING THE FULL $6500"

STEP 2
CONVERT TRAD-IRA TO A ROTH-IRA

THERE IS NO TIME LIMIT ON WHEN TO DO THE ROTH-IRA CONVERSION BUT BEST TO DO WITHIN 2-3 DAYS

STEP 3
WATCH OUT FOR THE PRO-RATA RULE

THE BALANCE OF ALL IRAS (TRADITIONAL, SIMPLE, SEP) MUST BE ZERO BY DECEMBER 31ST OF THE CONVERSION YEAR.
BASICALLY MUST CONVERT ALL IRA TO TO ROTH IRAS (WARNING: TAX EVENT) OR ROLL ANY LARGE IRA INTO YOUR 401KS

STEP 4
FILL OUT FORM 8606

EACH FORM MUST BE DONE FOR YOU AND YOUR SPOUSE ON YOUR TAX RETURN. THE LINE ON 15C AND 18 SHOULD BE ZERO ON YOUR TAX FORM.

STEP 5
REPEAT FOR NEXT YEAR

CONTINUE THIS PROCESS EVERY YEAR FOR MAX TAX-FREE GROWTH

REPEAT

Understanding the Pro-Rata Rule

While we won't delve too deeply, it's essential to note that the IRS mandates an end-of-year calculation that consolidates all your existing IRAs (like SEP, SIMPLE, and Traditional IRAs) into **ONE collective IRA account**. This rule can throw a wrench in the works if you're attempting a backdoor Roth conversion.

With the pro-rata rule in effect, the taxation of your Roth IRA depends on the ratio of all your total pre-tax IRA balances to the entirety of your IRA holdings. The only way to sidestep this is to **convert ALL your IRA accounts into your Roth IRA**, accepting the substantial tax bill that comes with it (given that with a Roth, you're paying taxes upfront to avoid future taxations on gains). Once you've transitioned to one consolidated Roth IRA, then you can safely do the backdoor Roth IRA.

Financial Tip

Caution: This is a complex area. If you possess other primary IRAs, such as SIMPLE or SEP IRA, it's advised to steer clear of attempting the backdoor Roth IRA due to the complications brought on by the pro-rata rule.

For those with existing IRAs like the SIMPLE or SEP IRA: It's pivotal to avoid the backdoor Roth IRA to prevent complications in your tax filings. But if you see your income approaching the limit for Roth IRA contributions, it's wise to consider the backdoor Roth IRA beforehand. And if any hiccups occur, reach out to your brokerage to help "re-characterize" your contributions.

Is the Backdoor Roth IRA Illegal?

Though some financial pundits have debated its intent, Congress officially sanctioned the backdoor Roth IRA for everyone in 2018. The Roth IRA, with its myriad of tools and benefits, is an effective way to diversify your retirement tax strategy.

Eager to delve deeper into the Backdoor Roth IRA? Refer to this Step-by-Step Guide for a more comprehensive understanding:

How to Do a Backdoor Roth with Vanguard/Fidelity via Step-by-Step Instructions	

Diving into the Health Savings Account (HSA)—Your "Stealth IRA"

Let's unveil the covert financial ninja: the Health Savings Account (HSA). If you're covered under a high-deductible health insurance plan, you have the option to set up an HSA independently or through your employer.

For 2023, the contribution ceilings are set at $3,850 for individuals and $7,750 for families.

One standout feature of the HSA is its **TRIPLE TAX ADVANTAGE,** where the funds are allocated toward medical expenses—an inevitability as we age. Moreover, the HSA serves as an alternative avenue to tuck away your money, shielded from taxes, thereby earning its moniker, the "Stealth IRA."

6 Noteworthy Benefits of the Health Savings Account (HSA)

- It's funded using pre-tax dollars, granting you an enticing tax deduction.

- The funds are readily accessible for any health-related expenses, without invoking taxes or a 10 percent penalty.

- Growth within the HSA isn't subjected to taxes, and you can make tax-free withdrawals for medical expenses.

- Past the age of sixty-five, you can freely withdraw from your HSA without any penalties, although non-medical withdrawals will be taxed as income.

- Unlike a Flexible Spending Account (FSA) or Health Reimbursement Account (HRA), there's no end-of-the-year rush to use up your HSA funds. Plus, your balance rolls over, even if you transition to a new job.

- The contributions can be funneled into mutual funds within the HSA, maximizing potential returns.

6 Retirement Scenarios for Doctors (2023)

Now that you've delved into the intricate world of retirement accounts, let's explore some real-life scenarios. These examples should help illustrate situations similar to your own. Our primary objective is to optimize the tax-efficient savings a doctor can allocate for retirement, based on their unique tax circumstances. For further clarity, refer back to the Retirement Account Chart as needed.

Doctor Case A: Full time employed W2 doctor with an income of $120,000 with an employer-sponsored Traditional 401K plan with 5% match.

 (1) Fund the Traditional 401K up to $22,500 with the 5% employer match (Additional $6,000)

 (2) Open a Traditional or Roth IRA (up to $6,500, max MAGI income limit is $153,000). We recommend Roth IRA route due to tax-free growth.

 (3) Dump the rest of his post-tax income paycheck into a Non-retirement Taxable brokerage account (No limit) with 15% long-term capital tax on any earnings.

 This W2 doctor is in great shape and can contribute a significant amount of his income to retirement in a tax-efficient manner.

Doctor Case B: Full time employed W2 doctor with an income of **$110,000,** but unfortunately her employer doesn't offer any Traditional 401K plans or any other SIMPLE IRA retirement plans. She does some casual fill-in at another optometry office and roughly has **$10,000 in 1099 income.**

 (1) Open a traditional or Roth IRA (up to $6,500, max income limit is $153,000). In this case, either route is okay due to the doctor's income bracket. But when in doubt, the tie goes to the Roth IRA.

 (2) Open Solo-401K for her 1099 income (max $22,500). It is harder to set up, but this will allow her to do a backdoor Roth-IRA if her income starts to rise past $153,000 limit in the future.

 (3) Dump the rest of her post-tax income paycheck into a Non-retirement Taxable brokerage account (No limit) with 15% long-term capital tax on any earnings.

 This W2 doctor has a significantly more limited max contribution to her retirement fund, compared to our Doctor A. It is great that she has some 1099 income on the side or else, the only thing that she can do is a Roth IRA.

 Doctor B can technically open a SEP-IRA for her 1099 income, but she can only contribute 25% of her total net 1099 income to the SEP IRA (Ex: only $2,500 can be contributed to her SEP IRA). She can deduct the 1099 contribution to SEP IRA when she files her end of year taxes. But it will prevent her from doing a backdoor Roth-IRA if her income starts to rise past $153,000 limit in the future.

Doctor Case C: Full time 1099 doctor with an income of $190,000, working for a private office where there is no employer-sponsored 401K or health benefits. She forms a S-Corp or LLC where she is both the employer/employee.

(1) Open a Solo-401K for her 1099 income, but she can contribute $22,500 of her total 1099 income to the Solo-401K. She is also allowed to do an employer's match up of up to $43,500 but it cannot exceed $66,000 total or Max 100% of her total income, whichever is less.

She can deduct the 1099 contribution to Solo-401K when she files her end of year taxes

(2) Open a Backdoor Roth IRA (up to $6,500, since max income limit is $140,000)

(3) Dump the rest of any post-tax income paycheck into a Non-retirement Taxable brokerage account (No limit) with 15% long-term capital tax on any earnings.

Since this Doctor C is all 1099 income with a high income, she should open a solo 401K account even though it takes more work to set up. This will allow her to do a backdoor Roth IRA. Technically, she can do a SEP IRA (similar contribution to Solo 401K) but it will complicate her tax situation when she tries to open her backdoor Roth IRA due to the Pro-Rata rule.

Doctor Case D: Full time Private Practice Business Owner Incorporated as LLC or S-Corp, and pay himself a W2 salary of $150,000

$ (1) Open an Employer-sponsored Traditional 401K for himself but must allow all his staff members to participate (Up to $22,500 contribution max) if desired. This usually haves slightly higher yearly management fee.

? (2) Consider a Defined Benefit Plan or Profit-Sharing plan (up to $265,000)

🏛 (3) Open a Backdoor Roth IRA (up to $6,500, since max income limit is $153,000)

📈 (4) Dump the rest of any post-tax income paycheck into a Non-retirement Taxable brokerage account (No limit) with 15% long-term capital tax on any earnings.

As private practice owner, you have the option to either pay yourself a salary as a W2 employee of your corporation or pay yourself as 1099 income independent. Being 1099 income allows you to still open a SIMPLE-IRA ($15,500) or SEP-IRA (25% of net, up to $66,000) but again would complicate you opening a backdoor Roth IRA. Also, you have the option to do a 401K with a profit-sharing plan ($20,500 401K with an employer's match up to $40,500, but $66,000 total (or max 100% of net income, whichever is less), or even a defined benefit plan ($265,000 max).

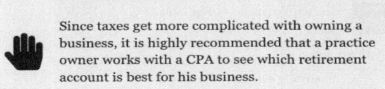

Since taxes get more complicated with owning a business, it is highly recommended that a practice owner works with a CPA to see which retirement account is best for his business.

Doctor Case E: Full time Employed Associates with a W2 salary of $150,000, with a Employer SIMPLE IRA at her office with a 3% Match. She does some 1099 fill-in of $20,000

(1) Fully Fund the SIMPLE IRA $15,500 with the 3% Match

(2) Open Solo-401K for her 1099 income (max $22,500). It is harder to set up, but this will allow her to do a backdoor Roth-IRA if her income starts to rise past the $153,000 limit in the future but she would need to rollover her SIMPLE IRA once she leave her job

(3) Dump the rest of any post-tax income paycheck into a Non-retirement Taxable brokerage account (No limit) with 15% long-term capital tax on any earnings.

Doctor E can technically open a SEP-IRA for her 1099 income, but she can only contribute 25% of her total net 1099 income to the SEP IRA (Ex: only $5,000 can be contributed to her SEP IRA). She can deduct the 1099 contribution to SEP IRA when she files her end of year taxes. Again but it will prevent her from doing a backdoor Roth-IRA if her income starts to rise past $153,000 limit in the future. I would go toward Solo-401K route because she would need it eventually anyway.

She can also open a Traditional IRA $6,500 but since she is over the MAGI income of $83,000, she won't be able to deduct it during tax, which defeats the whole purpose. She cannot do the Roth IRA $6,500 via Backdoor due to the pro rata Rule. So unfortunately, this OD is limited to her SIMPLE IRA as her only retirement, unless she has a health spending account (HSA)

Doctor Case F: Full time employed W2 doctor with an income of $120,000 with an employer-sponsored Traditional 401K plan with 5% match. Also married with a non-working Spouse and on a high-deductible medical plan (access to HSA)

 (1) Fund the Traditional 401K up to $22,500 with the 5% employer match (Additional $7,500)

 (2) Open a Roth IRA (up to $6,500, max income limit is $153,000, Married $228,000).

 (3) Open a Spousal Roth IRA (up to $6,500)

 (4) Fund the HSA (up to $3,850 Single, $7,750 Family). This will add as "triple tax-advantaged stealth IRA" later in life

 (5) Dump the rest of his post-tax income paycheck into a Non-retirement Taxable brokerage account (No limit) with 15% long-term capital tax on any earnings.

 This W2 doctor is in great shape and can contribute a significant amount of their income in addition to her non-working spousal to retirement in a tax-efficient manner, especially with that HSA

5 Steps to Building Wealth and Investing for the Long-Term

Now that you've honed your retirement planning skills, let's delve into actionable tips to effectively build wealth over the long term. Here are five pivotal steps for bolstering your retirement nest egg:

(1) **Automate Your Savings and Prioritize Yourself**

(2) **Embrace Low-cost Index Funds and Resist Market Timing**

(3) **Evade Exorbitant Funds Fees**

(4) **Reevaluate Your Savings Annually**

(5) **Boost Your Savings Rate Yearly**

(1) Pay Yourself by Automating Your Savings

Do you have friends who are perpetually worried about money woes and wonder about how they make it financially? Oftentimes, they're caught in the paycheck-to-paycheck grind.

Income levels, whether $50,000 or $120,000 annually, don't necessarily dictate wealth. It's about spending habits. For instance, a doctor with a $120,000 salary, splurging $130,000 on luxuries, has a negative net worth of $10,000. Such financial behavior can render someone poorer than an individual without a roof over their head.

Consider the doctor flaunting a swanky car and an opulent watch.

Chances are, he's wallowing in debt, destined to toil into his senior years, shackled by his lavish choices, far from financial freedom (a symptom sometimes called *golden handcuffs*).

Many fall prey to societal pressures, striving for the Instagram-perfect lifestyle. Alas, not everyone can live like a celebrity.

Many doctors make the mistake of prioritizing external financial commitments. They settle government dues, credit card bills, and loans, often leaving their personal savings as an afterthought. This misguided sequence often ends with a near-empty bank account, accompanied by complaints about saving woes.

How do the rich grow their wealth? By flipping this narrative. They PAY themselves first.

Before indulging in expenses, they automatically save a portion of their earnings toward retirement funds, debt repayment, or savings for short-term objectives. This disciplined approach makes sure you spend money wisely, helping you tell the difference between what you really need and what you just want.

It's a myth that living frugally is unattainable. For instance, statistics show that an individual in San Francisco, despite its steep living costs, requires merely around $13,368 annually (or $1,114 monthly) for basic necessities. Luxuries like Netflix or the latest iPhone aren't counted in these essentials.

Given this, optometrists, typically drawing a salary upwards of $130,000 annually, shouldn't find it challenging to save for retirement or expedite debt repayment. Here's the mantra to swear by:

PAY YOURSELF FIRST, your sixty-five-year-old self will be forever grateful.

On a doctor's paycheck, basic necessities are well within reach. Once essential expenses, retirement contributions, and savings are sorted, then you are welcome to spend guilt-free on whatever makes you happy.

Now, the key is to automate this process.

Achieving financial success demands initial effort. However, once investments and retirement accounts are operational, it's essentially an auto-pilot process. Most financial platforms facilitate automatic monthly transfers. The less you think about savings, the more natural it becomes to put yourself first.

Financial Tip:

Remember, rich people prioritize themselves. They proactively allocate a portion of their earnings to retirement funds, debt clearance, or short-term savings goals, ensuring a comfortable cushion for their future before indulging in immediate gratification.

---

(2) Embrace Passive, Low-Cost Index Funds and Resist Market Timing

It can indeed be unnerving to watch your retirement portfolio plunge by 30–40 percent within a year, as witnessed during the 2008–2009 Recession. Yet remember that the market has a history of bouncing back. When considering the long-term perspective, the stock market can indeed be an ally.

For those diversifying across stocks and bonds, **we typically advocate for a portfolio centered around the S&P 500 Stock Index.** This index reflects the performance of the top five hundred companies in the USA. On average, a fully stock-based portfolio can yield about a 10 percent return. But as one nears retirement and incorporates more bonds into the mix, a more conservative estimate might be closer to 7 percent.

Attempting to time the market is a fool's errand. Hence, we advise a continuous presence in the stock market, riding out its highs and lows.

Financial Tip

A diversified stocks and bonds portfolio, majorly focused on the S&P 500 stock index representing the USA's top five hundred companies, can anticipate an average return of approximately 10 percent for a predominantly stock-based portfolio.

---

(3) Avoid High Fees

The impact of fees can't be underestimated. Even fees that seem nominal can substantially erode your returns over an investment lifetime.

Which Fees Should You Watch Out For?

- **Asset Under Management (AUM) financial advisory fee:** Typically around 1-2 percent annually.

- **Loaded mutual funds:** These come with an added fee, sometimes as high as 5 percent, either levied upfront (Front-loaded) or after a set duration (Back-loaded).

- **Actively managed mutual funds:** These can carry fees up to 1 percent.

It's prudent to sidestep actively managed mutual funds with high expense ratios. If you're constrained by limited 401(k) options, ensure the cost is under 1 percent.

Consider this illustrative example

Two twenty-six-year-old newly graduated optometrists, Smart Sammy and Lazy Larry, both start with $25,000 in their IRA and contribute $10,000 annually, aiming for a 7 percent average yearly return over forty years.

Scenario 1: Smart Sammy opts for a low-cost index fund with Vanguard. In forty years, his projected retirement savings is about **$2,500,000**.

Scenario 2: Lazy Larry thinks, "A 1 percent AUM fee isn't a big deal," and brings a financial advisor on board. Assuming ethical practices, the advisor chooses the same index fund. In forty years, Larry's savings is approximately **$1,910,000** – a whopping $590,000 less than Sammy's. That's an average annual 1 percent advisory fee of $14,750 over forty years! All for what? The same index fund recommendation.

And there's more to ponder! To justify their fees, some advisors might over-complicate portfolios with costly front-loaded mutual funds or even pricier actively managed funds. This could mean fees as high as 8 percent when combining advisory costs with fund charges.

What Defines "Low-Cost"?

While a mutual fund with a 0.50 percent expense ratio is considered reasonable, the gold standard is below 0.20 percent. The silver lining? Major players like Fidelity and Vanguard now offer funds with fees as low as 0.10 percent or even zero.

In summary, fees matter! Stay informed and gravitate toward low-cost passive index funds whenever feasible.

(4) Annually Review Your Retirement Savings

While we advocate a steadfast and consistent investment approach, it's wise NOT to neglect your account. Due to the ebb and flow of the market, your initial asset allocation (the division of your funds among various stocks and bonds) will inevitably shift over time.

For instance, suppose you opted to allocate 70 percent to stock index funds and 30 percent to bonds at the start of 2019. However, market fluctuations might alter this distribution to 75 percent in stocks and 25 percent in bonds by year-end.

This is where rebalancing steps in – It corrects this misalignment, realigning to the initial 70 percent/30 percent allocation. Some investors rebalance with higher frequency (e.g., monthly, which can be overly frequent) or when a specific threshold is reached (e.g., when stocks constitute 40 percent of their portfolio).

> **We advocate for simplicity- Rebalancing your asset allocation ONCE a year is good enough.**

Fortunately, many 401(k) or IRA accounts facilitate this by allowing users to set their desired percentages for mutual funds in line with their stock and bond asset allocation. This ensures that rebalancing can be executed swiftly, often within minutes.

(5) Elevate Your Savings Rate Annually

Starting your retirement savings journey is arguably the most challenging step, but what follows is straightforward: progressively increase your savings rate each year. For example, should you receive a pay raise or bonus, consider allocating 25–50 percent of that increment to boost your retirement savings rate by 1–2 percent.

In reality, such a modest 1–2 percent annual increase in your retirement contribution goes largely unnoticed. However, its cumulative impact on your future financial stability is profound. Also, many 401(k) plans offer an auto-increase feature. Activate it!

Summary:

You made it to the end of this long chapter! While this material may not be applicable yet, you will be off to a running start when you get that big doctor paycheck.

We will leave you with some lasting thoughts. Frankly, the term *retirement* doesn't resonate well with us. It paints a picture of an idler lounging on a beach without any meaningful societal contribution.

Our goals are simple—to attain financial freedom.

This is a freedom that will enable us to pursue whatever stirs our souls without fretting over bills. This financial liberty empowers professionals, like doctors, who've invested years in education and dedication, to chase their genuine passions.

If your fantasy is to recline on a beach with a mai tai in hand, we say embrace it wholeheartedly! But if you wish to continue patient care, imagine the fulfillment in knowing you're aiding patients out of passion, not necessity.

Ultimately, investing for the future is about carving a path to financial freedom!

Key Takeaways:

- Begin with a clear understanding of your budget. Before diving into retirement savings, ensure you have an emergency fund covering three to six months of expenses, or prioritize paying off high-interest debts.

- A handy benchmark for retirement planning is: [25 x annual post-retirement expenses] = total needed in retirement funds. We advocate that all doctors amass a robust nest egg, aiming for at least $2 million.

- Embrace the power of compounding interest. The earlier you commence your retirement savings, the more this interest magnifies your capital growth. With any earned income, think about maximizing your Roth IRA contribution annually.

- Familiarize yourself with the array of retirement plans available to optometrists. Commonly, a blend of a 401(k) employer plan and a Roth IRA (typically through a backdoor due to income limits) is the chosen route.

- If your healthcare plan has a high deductible and offers a Health Savings Account (HSA) option, seize the opportunity to fully fund this triply tax-advantaged "stealth IRA."

- Always automate your savings. Pay yourself by setting aside retirement funds first. Remain committed to low-cost index funds and sidestep high fees. And remember, with each annual raise and bonus, increase your savings rate.

CHAPTER 14:

PREPARING FOR STUDENT LOAN DEBT AFTER GRADUATION | BY DAT BUI, OD

The rising costs of higher education coupled with the stress of paying student students are putting increasing on student's financial future.
—Hank Johnson

As of 2023, the student debt crisis in the United States has ballooned to a staggering $1.77 trillion, posing a societal epidemic that hampers the financial growth of many young professionals. This financial burden often forces newly minted doctors to live with their parents longer, unable to afford rent or even contemplate buying a home. Consequently, these financial pressures delay life milestones like starting a family, primarily because these young professionals struggle to manage their own finances.

While previous chapters have outlined strategies for significantly reducing the amount of student loans you may need to take— such as securing scholarships and living frugally—the unfortunate truth remains: the majority of doctors will graduate with substantial student loan debt.

Optometrists face an even bleaker financial picture. The average starting salary for new optometry graduates in 2023 stagnates at around $130,000, whereas the average student debt is rising, often exceeding $250,000—with some doctors accruing nearly $350,000 in debt. Therefore, it is crucial for optometry students to be acutely aware of these financial pitfalls and to formulate a robust student loan repayment plan as soon as they start drawing a doctor's salary

So what is the typical approach among optometrists? Many yield to societal expectations to maintain a "rich doctor lifestyle," relegating their student loans to the back burner. They make minimum payments over two decades or more, hoping for a miraculous loan forgiveness from the government after twenty to twenty-five years. Unfortunately, this is the norm, and the norm falls short. A "normal" approach won't lead to wealth or remarkable success.

Let's change this narrative. This chapter will guide you through taking control of your financial destiny, specifically concerning your student loans after graduation.

Step 1: Understand the Extent of Your Loan Debt

First, you must be fully aware of the amount of student loan debt you have incurred—from undergraduate through optometry school. Most of your loans will likely be federal loans, accessible through the Department of Education. You can easily review all your federal loan information using the National Student Loan Data System (NSLDS), which provides a comprehensive, national record of all your loans and grants, including balances, interest rates, servicers, and loan durations.

Access this information through the Federal Student Loan Repayment website (https://studentloans.gov) using your Federal Student Aid (FSA) ID. For any private loans, consult www.annualcreditreport.com to view all your outstanding debts.

Step 2: Identify the Type of Student Loan

Private Student Loans: These are usually more expensive, with higher interest rates that can exceed 10 percent. Interest accrues even while you're in school. Essentially, these loans are treated like consumer credit debt or business loans and usually require a good credit score or a co-signer if your credit score is poor.

Federal Student Loans: These are generally less expensive, with average interest rates around 6.8 percent, and come with multiple government program benefits. Federal loans also have a grace period that allows you to defer payments while you're in school—at least as a half-time student. If your federal loans are subsidized, the government will cover the interest during your school years.

SUBSIDIZED FEDERAL LOANS	UNSUBSIDIZED FEDERAL LOANS
Do not accrue interest while in school, during grace period or deferment	Accrue interest while in school, during grace period or deferment
Direct Subsidized: Only for undergraduate	**Direct Unsubsidized:** Loans that accrue interest during all periods
Direct Consolidation Combination of all subsidized loans into a weighted interest rate and one monthly payment	Direct Consolidation Combination of all subsidized loans into a weighted interest rate and one monthly payment
Perkins: School-based loans for student with financial needs	Direct PLUS: Available to graduate or professional students that accrue interest during all periods and usually have higher interest than Direct Unsubsidized.
Subsidized FFEL- Loans dispersed prior to 2019 and is not eligible for forgiveness	Unsubsidized FFEL- Similar, but always accrue interest

Step 3: Choose the Repayment Strategy That Best Suits You

There are five primary strategies for repaying optometry school loans, each with its own set of implications and advantages. These include the following:

- (I) Tuition Reimbursement Program

- (II) Standard Federal Payment Plan

- (III) Federal Loan Forgiveness Program (Ten-Year Public Service Loan Forgiveness)

- (IV) Federal Loan Forgiveness Program (Twenty- to Twenty-Five-Year Total Forgiveness)

- (V) Aggressive Debt Payback Through Student Loan Refinancing

Let's dive into each of these options in more detail:

(I) Tuition Reimbursement Programs

Tuition reimbursement programs are employer benefits wherein the employer allocates a set amount of "free" money as a part of your salary benefits toward your student loans, usually in exchange for a commitment to work for a specific number of years.

Some programs might require you to contribute a certain amount, which they then match or reimburse. We explored these in chapter 4, "How to Pay for School," but here's a **quick review:**

Military Health Professions Scholarship Programs

Though called a "scholarship," the Military's Health Professions Scholarship Program (HPSP) is more aptly described as a contract. This program covers tuition, fees, and necessary expenses while providing a taxable living stipend—about $2,200 per month as of 2023. In return, you commit to a year of active military service for each year you receive this funding. Be aware that military optometrists usually earn less than their civilian peers and must adapt to military governance over various aspects of their professional and personal lives.

Indian Health Service (IHS) Programs

Similarly, the Indian Health Service (IHS) offers what is called a "scholarship" but is essentially a contract. Eligibility is limited to members of a federally recognized American Indian tribe or Alaska Native village. The program provides a monthly living stipend (at least $1,500 as of 2023) and covers all tuition and fees. In return, you commit to one year of service for each year of scholarship support, with a minimum of two years, serving primarily Native American communities.

Corporate Employer Loan Repayment Programs

Some private employers in the optometry sector, such as LensCrafters, National Vision (also known as America's Best), and Walmart Optometry, offer loan repayment programs. These programs partially cover tuition and generally last between two and four years. While this benefit may be taxable, some recent legislation allows a portion to be tax-free for the employee and tax-deductible for the employer.

Bear in mind that these programs are often seen by employers as an alternative to a higher salary rather than an additional benefit. However, they could serve as a negotiation point when you're seeking your first job post-graduation. Often, these programs come with specific location requirements, frequently in more rural areas.

By understanding these options, you'll be better equipped to choose a repayment route that aligns with both your career goals and financial needs.

(II) Standard Federal Payment Plan

If you're not eligible for tuition reimbursement or loan forgiveness programs, then your primary option is to pay off your student loans outright. You can either do this through a federal repayment program or take the arguably smarter route of refinancing into private loans for a lower interest rate (as discussed later on in this chapter).

Unlike some other repayment options, there's no prescribed timeline for paying off these loans. You could technically pay them off immediately (though this is unlikely unless you have wealthy parents or win the lottery), or you can stretch the payments out for as long as you'd like—up to a maximum of thirty years. The length of time you choose will influence your monthly payments, which are also determined by the type of repayment plan you select.

If you're like most optometrists, you likely financed your optometry education (or perhaps even your undergraduate education) through federal loans, serviced by organizations like Nelnet, Great Lakes Education Loan Services Inc., Navient, or FedLoan Servicing, to name a few.

While you can manage multiple monthly payments to different servicers, a more efficient first step would be to consolidate these loans through a direct consolidation loan.

Understanding the Difference: Consolidation vs. Refinancing

Consolidation enables you to combine all your federal student loans into a single loan under a federal lender, simplifying the repayment process with just one monthly payment. The interest rate for the consolidated loan is an average of the rates on the loans you are bringing together, meaning your final rate could be a bit higher or lower than your current rates. The key benefit of consolidation is the convenience of having a single monthly payment to manage.

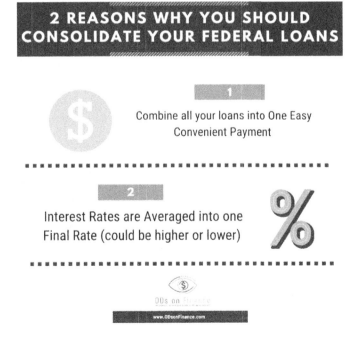

2 REASONS WHY YOU SHOULD CONSOLIDATE YOUR FEDERAL LOANS

1

Combine all your loans into One Easy Convenient Payment

2

Interest Rates are Averaged into one Final Rate (could be higher or lower)

ODs on Finance
www.ODsonFinance.com

Financial Tip

It's important to distinguish this from refinancing your student loans. Refinancing typically involves consolidating all your federal loans into a single private loan payment, usually at a lower interest rate. However, once you refinance, you are effectively exiting the federal loan program, and you'll lose any federal benefits that come with it. Refinancing is a definitive decision that should be made carefully, considering the trade-offs involved.

Federal Loan Repayment Plans

Plan	Payments Type	TERM	Eligibility
Standard	Fixed	10 years	All Federal Direct Loans
Graduated	Payment starts low and increase over time	10-30 years	All Federal Direct Loans
Extended Fixed	Fixed	Up to 25 years	All Federal Direct Loans
Extended Graduated	Payment starts low and increase over time	Up to 25 years	All Federal Direct Loans

Income-Driven Plan

Plan	Payments Type	TERM	Eligibility	% of Poverty Income Exception	Married Filing Jointly	Married Filing Separately	NOTES
SAVE (Saving on a Valuable Education)	5% of Discretionary income if all undergrad, **10%** if graduate. Otherwise weighted average if both	**20 years** - all undergrad; **25 years** - any grad; 10 years for low balance borrowers (<$12,000)	All Federal Direct Loans except for Parent Plus Loans	225%	Joint income	Only borrowers' income. Exclude spouse from family size.	**Any interest NOT covered by calculated payment is waived**
REPAYE (Revised Pay As You Earn Repayment Plan)	10% of Discretionary income	20 years - all undergrad; 25 years - any grad	All Federal Direct Loans except for Parent Plus Loans	225%	Joint income	Only borrowers' income. Exclude spouse from family size.	Will fully converted to SAVE after 7/30/23
PAYE (Pay As You Earn Repayment Plan)	10% of Discretionary income but never more than the 10-year standard plan	**Up to 20 years**	All Federal Direct Loans except for Parent Plus Loans. You must have taken out your first Federal loan after 9/30/2007, and received a loan disbursement after 9/30/2011	150%	Joint income	Only borrowers' income. Exclude spouse from family size.	Must choose before July 1, 2024
IBR (Income-based)	10-15% of Discretionary income	20-25 years	Lesser of 20% of Discretionary income or amount for fixed payment over 12 years, whichever is less	150%	Joint income	Only borrowers' income. Exclude spouse from family size.	
ICR (Income-Contingent)	Lesser of 20% of Discretionary income or amount for fixed payment over 12 years, whichever is less	**Up to 25 years**	Direct Loans including Parent Plus Loans (only one)	100%	Joint income	Only borrowers' income. Exclude spouse from family size.	Cannot choose after 7/1/2024 unless have Parent Plus Loans (PPL)

Types of Federal Loan Payment Programs Explained

Standard repayment plan: This plan is generally set to a default term of ten years but can be extended up to twenty-five years (known as the *extended repayment plan*). It involves consistent monthly payments and usually accrues the least amount of interest over a ten-year repayment period.

Graduated repayment plan: In this plan, your payments start out low and gradually increase over the life of the loan. That means you'll be making the highest payments toward the end of the repayment term.

Income-contingent repayment plan (ICR): Similar to IBR, this plan offers a monthly payment that's either 20 percent of your discretionary income or a fixed amount based on a twelve-year repayment plan, whichever is lower.

Income-based repayment plan (IBR): Here, your monthly payments will be between 10 percent and 15 percent of your discretionary income and will be recalibrated each year based on your income and family size. Note that if you're married, your spouse's income will be included in the calculation.

Pay-as-you-earn repayment plan (PAYE): Like REPAYE, this plan caps your maximum monthly payment at 10 percent of your discretionary income. Your payments will actually be lower if you have a high debt-to-income ratio, but they won't exceed what you'd pay on the standard repayment plan.

Revised pay-as-you-earn repayment plan (REPAYE): This plan sets your monthly payments at 10 percent of your discretionary income but will be phased out and replaced by SAVE after July 30, 2023.

SAVE (Saving on a Valuable Education): This is the newest income-driven repayment (IDR) plan, and all REPAYE borrowers will automatically transition to it. SAVE has several significant benefits for optometrists:

- It offers a 100 percent interest subsidy on any accruing interest, meaning if your payments don't cover the interest, you won't be responsible for the interest that accrues. This is particularly beneficial for lower-income borrowers.

- If married, you can exclude your spouse's income by filing taxes separately.

- The income exclusion for payment calculation increases from 150 percent to 225 percent of the poverty income level.

- **Note:** *Discretionary income* is what you earn above 150 percent of the federal poverty level for your family size. If you're married, your spouse's income will be counted, which will increase your monthly payment.

- In essence, SAVE only charges 5 percent of your discretionary income for undergraduate loans and 10 percent for graduate loans. If you have both, a weighted average will apply.

Financial Tip

Confused by all these income-driven plans? Don't worry. Usually during your school exit interview, choosing SAVE or PAYE is the recommended route. If you're aiming for total federal loan forgiveness, SAVE generally results in the lowest total payments over twenty-five years, whereas PAYE offers a shorter forgiveness term of twenty years. However, if you plan to refinance your student loans or are considering the ten-year public service loan forgiveness (PSLF) program, then SAVE is the way to go.

---

3 Notable Benefits of Federal Programs:

I'd like to spotlight some significant perks associated with federal loan programs:

1. **Flexible repayment plans:** These plans can be easily modified during financial hardships, a feature that's particularly helpful for doctors who may experience fluctuations in income.

2. **Total forgiveness:** If a borrower who has no co-signer either passes away or becomes fully or partially disabled, all federal loans will be entirely forgiven. However, it's important to note that declaring bankruptcy won't lead to loan dismissal. In such cases, the government retains the authority to garnish future earnings.

3. **No need for good credit to consolidate:** Unlike private refinancing, where your credit score could substantially impact your interest rate, the federal government offers

consolidation at the same rate for everyone.

This can be beneficial for doctors with poor credit scores, although it might feel frustrating for those who have maintained excellent credit.

(III) Federal Loan Forgiveness Program (Ten-Year Public Service Loan Forgiveness or PSLF)

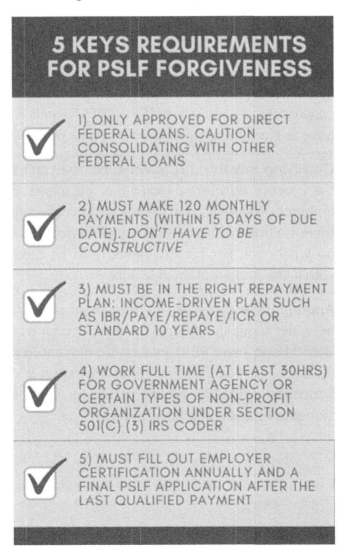

Initiated in October 2007, doctors who work for a non-profit organization for ten years can have their student loans fully forgiven, provided all requirements are met, and without incurring a tax bill.

Let's delve into the specific PSLF requirements in more detail:

1. **Qualified federal direct loans only:** Perkins Loans are technically ineligible, but you can make them eligible by consolidating them through a direct consolidation loan.

a. **Caution:** If you've been making standard ten-year or income-driven qualified payments and then decide to consolidate, you've just reset your PSLF timeline and will have to start the ten-year period all over again.

2. **Qualifying monthly 120 payments:** You can't expedite the process by making additional payments or larger amounts. Payments don't have to be consecutive, so if there's a gap in your full-time employment, you can pick up where you left off. Payments must be made in full within fifteen days of the due date.

3. **Appropriate income-driven repayment plan:** You must be under a qualifying repayment plan, such as Income-Based Repayment (IBR), Income-Contingent Repayment (ICR), Pay As You Earn (PAYE) or **Saving on a Valuable Education (SAVE)**. Payments under the ten-year standard repayment plan also qualify.

Financial Tip

Don't opt for the standard ten-year standard repayment plan, as it's the most expensive choice for any forgiveness program. Remember, our goal is to pay the least amount possible over ten years. SAVE or PAYE is recommended.

---

4. **Full-time employment:** You must work full-time (at least thirty hours per week) for a government agency or certain types of non-profit organizations under Section 501(c)(3) of the IRS code.

5. **No tax bill:** Unlike twenty- or twenty-five-year total forgiveness, there will be no tax bill at the end of PSLF.

Financial Tip

Not all non-profit organizations qualify for PSLF; they must also be tax-exempt, so check with your HR department. But as of August 2023, Kaiser optometrists, especially those in Texas and California, now qualify as employees of a non-profit organization and can thus apply for the ten-year PSLF program.

If you are one of the fortunate optometrists who qualify for the ten-year public service loan forgiveness (PSLF) program, this is usually the most financially prudent option. Just ensure you meet all the requirements and adhere to them for a decade. Be cautious, though, as some non-profit organizations are notorious for limiting associates to part-time hours—under twenty-eight per week—to avoid offering benefits, which could disqualify you from the program, or worse: letting you go unexpectedly prior to the ten years.

(IV) Federal Loan Forgiveness Program (Twenty- to Twenty-Five Year Total Forgiveness)

In the total student loan forgiveness program, also known as *income-driven repayment* (IDR), forgiveness typically kicks in after twenty or twenty-five years of qualified payments under certain income-driven repayment plans like PAYE or SAVE. **The great thing about this program is that you can work for any employer, non-profit or private.**

After making 240 or 300 qualified monthly payments (twenty or twenty-five years, depending on the specific plan), any remaining loan balance is forgiven. It's crucial to note that under current law, the **forgiven amount is considered taxable income**, so you may face a "tax bomb" at the end of the repayment period. However, this does allow you to ultimately avoid paying the full balance of your loans, especially if your monthly payments are relatively low compared to your initial loan amount.

The program is especially beneficial for borrowers who have high debt levels compared to their income, as it allows for smaller monthly payments stretched over a longer period of time, culminating in loan forgiveness.

If you are pursuing a total federal loan forgiveness program, we recommend two paths:

- **Pay As You Earn (PAYE):** twenty years of income-driven payment (or 240 payments)

- **Saving on a Valuable Education (SAVE):** twenty-five years of income-driven payment (or three hundred payments).

We recommend this one since it offers a 100 percent interest subsidy on any accruing interest, meaning if your payments don't cover the interest, you won't be responsible for the interest that accrues. This is particularly beneficial in reducing the massive tax bill at the end of twenty-five years.

STUDENT LOAN FORGIVENESS

Public Service Loan Forgiveness (PSLF)		Total Student Loan Forgiveness
10 years or 120 qualified payments made	DURATION TIME	20-25 years or 240-300 qualified depending on plan
Income-driven plans such as IBR, ICR, PAYE, REPAYE	REPAYMENT PLAN	Income-driven plans such as IBR, ICR, PAYE, REPAYE
Government, 501(c) (3) organizations or some non-tax exempt non-profits	EMPLOYER	Any employer
Direct Federal	LOANS	Direct Federal
Nope!	TAX BILL DUE?	Any amount forgiven will be taxed as ordinary income

Three Situations Where Student Loan Forgiveness Might Make Sense for Optometrists

Although we generally don't advocate for loan forgiveness, there are three specific situations that we frequently encounter where it might be advisable for optometrists to consider this option for their own financial well-being:

- **(1) 10-Year PSLF Forgiveness:** This option is suitable for optometrists who work full-time for 501(c) organizations or government agencies like Veterans Affairs, Indian Health Service, Kaiser, or academic non-profits and are fully committed to staying in such employment for a minimum of ten years. It's crucial to be fully aware of all program requirements, maintain meticulous records, and keep consistent contact with FedLoan Servicing.

- **(2) 20-25 Year Total Forgiveness for High-Risk Medical Conditions:** This path may be particularly relevant for optometrists who have existing high-risk medical conditions that make them susceptible to partial or full disability, or even early death. This becomes even more pressing if they don't qualify for disability or life insurance due to a lack of prior coverage. Those pursuing this route should also start saving for a substantial tax bill that would come due if the loans are forgiven and they are still alive after twenty to twenty-five years.

- **(3) 20-25 Year Total Forgiveness for High Debt-to-Income Ratio:** This option could be beneficial for optometrists with a debt-to-income ratio of 2.5:1 or greater.

While it's not impossible for an optometrist earning $100,000 to pay off a staggering $300,000 in student loans, doing so would require an extremely tight budget (think beans and rice) and serious retirement savings, and would likely take much longer than five to ten years to achieve.

In instances where the debt feels insurmountable, this could be a way out. However, if you are in this situation, you should also consider refinancing options in the future if your financial situation improves—such as moving to a lower cost-of-living state or receiving a salary increase. Additionally, you should start saving for the sizable tax bill that will come due upon loan forgiveness.

Like any rule of thumb, there are always exceptions. Numerous optometrists in our ODs on Finance community with substantial loan debts have achieved the seemingly impossible feat of paying off their student loans within just five years through diligent work and frugal living.

Personal Anecdotal

Speaking from personal experience, I was one of those optometrists who defied the odds. When I was a new graduate in 2015, working in the Bay Area of California, I earned a measly $85,000 a year while shouldering a $250,000 loan debt. This situation placed me in a debt-to-income (DTI) ratio of roughly 3:1, which, by conventional wisdom, should have led me to opt for federal loan forgiveness.

However, determined not to carry the burden of student loans for twenty or more years, I sought out as many fill-in jobs as I could. This hustle gradually increased my annual salary from

---

> $85,000 in my first year to $175,000 by my fourth year.
>
> By living frugally and below my means, I managed to pay off my loan in just 4.5 years. At the same time, I saved a significant amount for retirement and a down payment on a house. Both I and many of our ODs on Finance members serve as living proof that conquering massive debt is possible with the right mindset and hard work.

Should I Pursue 20-25 Year Total Student Loan Forgiveness?

Let's delve into whether you should even consider student loan forgiveness. At ODs on Finance, we personally advocate for every optometrist to take charge of their own financial destiny, rather than depending on government policies to shape their financial choices—especially for a span of twenty-five-plus years. With that bias acknowledged, we view 20-25 year total student loan forgiveness as a last resort for the following reasons:

(1) **Extended debt burden:** Staying in debt for two decades can be emotionally draining and could potentially impact your creditworthiness. This, in turn, affects other financial endeavors, like qualifying for a mortgage, practice loan, or car loan.

(2) **Interest accumulation:** Over a period of twenty years, interest on your loans will accumulate, possibly causing you to repay a much larger sum than the original loan amount.

(3) **Tax liability:** Under current tax laws, the amount forgiven after a twenty-year repayment term is

considered taxable income. This means you could face a substantial tax bill in the year your debt is forgiven.

Consider this: you'll still need to pay tax on any forgiven loan, which can be a hefty financial burden. Let's break it down with an example:

Dr. Normal has a typical student loan debt of $250,000 at an interest rate of 6.8 percent. She earns a $100,000 salary and opts for an income-driven repayment plan like PAYE, aiming for twenty-year loan forgiveness. Her monthly payments start at $818 in the first year and gradually increase to $1,434 by the twentieth year, based on her rising annual income.

After twenty years, here are some key figures:

- **Total forgiven balance:** $326,321

- **Total payments made:** $263,679 (higher than her original $250,000 loan)

- **Tax liability on forgiven debt (assuming a ~40 percent tax bracket for doctors):** $130,538

In total, she would end up paying $394,207—almost 1.57 times the original loan amount—over two decades.

---

(4) Complex federal eligibility requirements: Like with any federal forgiveness programs, 20-25 year options come with their own specific, and sometimes intricate, eligibility requirements. You'll need to certify your income annually and maintain consistent communication with your federal servicers each month to ensure that all 240+ payments are verified.

If you've ever tried to call your federal loan service provider for help, you'll often find yourself on hold for hours.

For instance, in 2019, we noticed that professionals who started the 10-year PSLF program back in October 2007 should have had their loans forgiven by October 2017. Despite extensive searches across news outlets and financial blogs, we found only ONE person who achieved loan forgiveness through PSLF. We did, however, find multiple lawsuits against loan providers for misleading borrowers about what counts as a non-profit or delaying qualifying payments. Essentially, these professionals are left in limbo, needing to restart their loan payments with nothing to show for their past five to ten years of payments.

Fast-forward to 2023, and we're seeing gradual approvals due to Biden's overhaul of the PSLF ten-year program to fix some glitches.

While improvements have been made to the forgiveness program, it continues to leave many borrowers frustrated and confused.

(5) **Changing legislative policies:** Government policies and loan forgiveness programs are susceptible to changes. Legislation or program adjustments could affect your eligibility or loan forgiveness terms. There have been numerous proposals to limit the ten-year PSLF to just $57,000 or even eliminate it altogether. Though it would require congressional action, this could indeed happen in the future.

Economically speaking, the first wave of twenty- to twenty-five-year total forgiveness will start rolling in by

2027.

Given the over $1.7 trillion in potential student debt to be forgiven, this could be a perfect financial storm in the making.

(6) **Career fulfillment and satisfaction:** Committing to twenty to twenty-five years in a specific employment setting solely for loan forgiveness could lead to job dissatisfaction if the role doesn't align with your career or personal interests.

In light of these complexities, optometrists should thoughtfully evaluate their long-term financial and career aspirations before committing to a twenty- to twenty-five-year federal loan forgiveness program. *The takeaway is simple: life is unpredictable, no matter how well-prepared you think you are.* Remaining in debt for twenty to twenty-five years could severely limit your opportunities for wealth-building.

Financial Tip:

If you are pursuing twenty- to twenty-five-year federal forgiveness, set aside any preconceptions about debt payoff. The objective of this program is to **make the minimum required payment based on your AGI income throughout its duration**. Think of it as a tax bill; aim not to pay the IRS more than what's due. In other words, avoid leaving a tip.

That said, it's advisable to consult with a student loan financial planner. (Recommended financial advisors can be found at https://odsonfinance.com/financial-advisors.) Get a flat-fee consultation and aim to touch base with them every two to three years. This ensures you remain on track,

---

especially given the ever-evolving nature of student loans.

⚠ It's imperative to be well-informed and mentally ready to commit to this journey, as twenty to twenty-five years is a significant period. The worst thing would be to change your mind after five years. Begin setting aside funds for the massive tax bill you'll face at the end of the twenty to twenty-five years in a separate brokerage account.

(VI) Aggressive Debt Payback through Student Loan Refinancing

Alright, now that we've covered the less common options for tackling student loan debt, let's dive into the approach that applies to **at least 85 percent of optometrists**: paying off student loans the traditional way.

Optometrists often accrue debt from both federal and private lenders to finance their education, leading to an average debt load of $220,000. Most of these loans are federal and come with average interest rates ranging from 5.5 percent to 6.8 percent.

The majority of optometrists end up refinancing their student loans to save thousands of dollars in interest. So, here's what you need to know about the student loan refinancing process, including an understanding of how underwriting works.

What Is Student Loan Refinancing?

Student loan refinancing involves securing a new loan from a private lender to replace your existing loans. This new loan comes with different interest rates and repayment terms. By refinancing with a private lender, you alter the existing conditions of your loan, especially concerning the interest rate and the repayment timeline.

Refinancing is free, can be repeated multiple times, and often results in significant savings through lower interest rates. Many lenders also offer sign-up cash bonuses for new clients.

It's important to differentiate this from federal direct consolidation. The latter essentially combines multiple loans into a single loan with an average, weighted interest rate. This can simplify the repayment process by making it easier to keep track of your debt. Federal Loan programs usually offer this consolidation option.

In summary, when you refinance your student loans, you're essentially consolidating multiple federal loans into a single loan, but you're doing so at a more favorable interest rate.

8 Reasons Why You Should Consider Refinancing Your Student Loans

(1) Significant Savings Due to Lower Interest Rates

Interest rates can range from 2.5 percent to 4.9 percent, depending on various factors, such as the lender, term duration, and whether the interest rate is variable or fixed.

Example: A typical optometrist might have a $200,000 loan at a 6.8 percent interest rate.

By refinancing to a rate of 2.5 percent, they could save $8,600 in interest during the first year alone. Over a twenty-year term, the total interest savings could amount to $112,049—that's more than half the principal!

(2) Cash Bonuses

Many banks offer a cash bonus of up to $1,200 for signing up for refinancing, adding to your savings.

(3) Simple Online Application and Superior Customer Service

Most applications can be easily submitted online, provided you have all the necessary financial documents. The entire process usually takes between 2-3 weeks. Additionally, private lenders generally offer better customer service than federal lenders, as they're keen to retain your business.

(4) Selective Refinancing and Repeated Applications

You don't have to refinance all your loans; you can choose which ones to refinance based on their interest rates. Furthermore, if your credit score improves or interest rates drop, you can refinance again to get even better rates. Unlike home mortgage refinancing, student loan refinancing doesn't come with origination fees, making it a cost-free endeavor.

Financial Tip

Because refinancing is free, many optometrists are *"refi-hacking"* multiple times by switching between lenders to capitalize on sign-up bonuses. Just remember to meet the minimum loan requirement for the cash bonus and to wait 90 days for it to be paid out.

---

(5) Best Deals Often Involve Short Terms and Variable Rates

For the lowest interest rates (typically between 2-3 percent), you'll likely need to commit to a 5-year term and choose a variable rate. However, be cautious: if federal rates spike, so could your monthly payments. Most optometrists end up opting for a 10-year fixed term with a slightly higher interest rate but better monthly cash flow.

(6) Eligibility Requirements

Private lenders usually require a minimum credit score of 700, proof of full-time income, and a reasonable debt-to-income ratio (often 2.5 to 1). These requirements can vary but will affect your eligibility and the rate you're offered.

(7) Flexibility in Financial Planning

Refinancing offers flexibility, whether you're looking to aggressively pay off debt or manage cash flow. Those focused on rapid debt payoff can select shorter terms, like 5 or 10 years, and aim to meet their financial goals within that time frame.

If you're juggling multiple financial goals, such as buying a home or starting a practice, longer terms like 15 or 20 years might be more suitable. Either way, extra payments can be made without penalties.

(8) Additional Perks: Forbearance and Loan Discharge

Given the competitive market, most private refinance lenders offer military deferment, hardship forbearance, and even full loan discharge in the event of death or disability—features that bring them closer in line with federal loan offerings.

As always, it's advisable to consult directly with potential lenders to confirm these benefits.

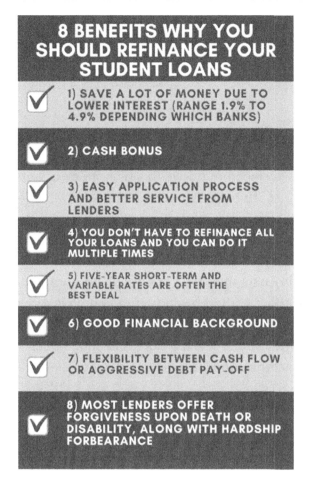

7 Negative Factors to Consider When Refinancing Your Student Loans

While we're big advocates for using lower interest rates to aggressively pay down your student loans, we also want to make you aware of certain situations where refinancing may NOT be the best idea.

(1) Eligibility for the Ten-Year PSLF Program

If you're an optometrist employed by a VA or non-profit and

intend to stay there for ten years, you should already be in a ten-year PSLF (Public Service Loan Forgiveness) program. In that case, stick to your original plan and avoid changing course midway.

(2) High Debt-to-Income Ratio, Typically 2.5:1 or Higher

If your debt-to-income ratio is this high, think about enrolling in a twenty- to twenty-five-year income-driven federal loan forgiveness program and making income-driven payments for the time being. This is particularly important when, for example, you're earning a salary of $100,000 but facing a debt of $300,000. In such situations, it's tough to aggressively pay off the debt without compromising retirement investments or other financial goals. However, remember that your financial landscape may shift. As you progress in your career, your income is likely to increase and your debt to decrease.

Example: Let's say your salary jumps to $130,000 and your debt shrinks to $270,000 after a year of payments.

This improves your debt-to-income ratio to 2:1, making it a good time to consider refinancing at a lower rate.

(3) Transitory or Unstable Financial Periods

Only consider refinancing if you have a stable, full-time job or at least five consistent days of part-time work per week. For new graduates, it's wise to wait at least three to six months before seeking refinancing options. If you're a current resident, your income may be too low to secure a favorable rate. For all other significant life events—such as an expected pregnancy, job loss, or transition to a new job—we highly recommend waiting until your situation stabilizes.

(4) Loss of Federal Repayment Benefits

Refinancing to a private loan means forfeiting federal benefits like hardship forbearance and loan deferment. Missing even one payment on a private loan can result in automatic default and a significant credit score drop, which is crucial to consider if you're planning to apply for a home mortgage or business loan. However, some private lenders like SoFi and Laurel Road do offer deferment and temporary forbearance options.

(5) No Federal Forgiveness for Partial or Full Disability or Death

If you're at high risk for disability or have a life-threatening condition, we 100 percent recommend sticking with federal loans. This is because obtaining adequate life or disability insurance may not be possible.

However, many private lenders now offer forgiveness upon death or disability. If yours doesn't, ensure you have adequate disability and life insurance before proceeding with refinancing.

(6) Student Debt Becomes Consumer Debt

Refinanced student loans, much like credit card debt, can be fully discharged in a Chapter 7 bankruptcy. However, the downside is that lenders can claim any remaining debt from your estate value—like 401(k), IRA, or rental investments—if you pass away, potentially leaving less for your heirs.

(7) Spousal Co-Signing Risks

If your spouse co-signs during the refinancing process, the loan won't disappear if you die; it becomes their debt. We typically don't recommend co-signing unless both parties are fully aware of the associated risks or the financial situation is exceptionally dire. However, many private lenders do offer a co-signer release upon death, so it's worth checking your lender's policies. There you have it, seven potential downsides to consider when thinking about refinancing your student loans.

7 Steps to Refinance Your Federal Loans

So you're considering refinancing your student loans. In simple terms, you'll need to find lenders offering lower interest rates, compare them, and then apply. Once approved, your new lender will pay off your existing loans, and you'll begin making monthly payments to them. But let's delve deeper into the seven steps involved in this process.

- ### Step 1: Determine the Loan Amount to Refinance

  Most doctors prefer to refinance the entire loan amount for simplicity and to consolidate payments. Plus, doing so usually comes with a bonus—around $1,000 if the loan amount exceeds $150,000.

- ### Step 2: Obtain Quick Online Rate Quotes from Multiple Lenders (Soft Credit Pull)

  At first glance, many student loan refinance lenders seem very similar. However, each has its own underwriting requirements and restrictions, which could affect your personal situation differently.

For instance, if you're on a student visa or green card, only specific lenders like SoFi might approve you, but they'll likely charge a higher interest rate. If your credit score is subpar (below 740), certain banks will penalize you with higher rates.

Therefore, it's essential to get rate estimates from at least two to three lenders. This is generally a quick process, taking about two to three minutes for an online pre-approval. These estimates will give you a sense of the market rate you might qualify for from different lenders.

While you're shopping around, some lenders might ask you to pre-qualify by providing basic information to estimate the rate you could get. Others may only show you a rate after you submit a full application, which then becomes an actual offer.

Note that a soft credit pull for pre-qualification typically doesn't affect your credit score. However, submitting an actual application will require a hard credit check, which could temporarily lower your credit score.

Financial Tip

We recommend starting your search with **Splash** and **Credible,** as their platforms cover about 90 percent of all refinance banks out there. After that, get at least one to two more quotes from lenders like Earnest, SoFi, or Laurel Road. This approach will give you a comprehensive view of your personal market rate across all lenders, based on your unique financial background, including credit score, debt-to-income ratio, and work history. Every month or so, we share an OD on Finance promo with our community, highlighting which

---

> lenders are currently offering the lowest rates.

- **Step 3: Choose Your Loan Duration and Interest Rate Type**

  Selecting a shorter loan duration, like five years instead of ten years, will net you a better interest rate, but your monthly payment will be much higher.

  Example: On a $200,000 student loan, a five-year loan at 1.95 percent would require a monthly payment of $3,501, versus $1,894 for a ten-year loan at 2.6 percent—a significant difference.

  While the allure of a lower interest rate is strong, it's crucial to ensure that the required monthly payment fits your budget. We typically recommend starting with a safer ten-year term. You can always make extra payments with no penalty or refinance to a shorter term later if your situation changes.

  A fixed rate remains constant over the life of the loan, which is ideal if you anticipate interest rates rising. A variable rate may start lower but can fluctuate based on federal rate changes. If you're planning to pay off your loans quickly—in three to five years—a variable rate might be acceptable.

Financial Tip

If you aim for aggressive loan payoff, consider a shorter five-year fixed term to get the lowest rate and higher monthly payments. This strategy is effective if you're willing to live frugally, like a student, for five years. On the other hand, if you have other financial goals, such as buying a home or starting a practice, a longer ten-year or fifteen-year fixed term could offer better cash flow and savings options.

For most doctors, we recommend a ten-year fixed rate as a balanced approach.

- **<u>Step 4: Complete the Full Application and Gather Required Documents (Hard Credit Pull)</u>**

   Even if you're pre-qualified, you'll still need to submit a full application to proceed. You'll be asked for more in-depth information and supporting documents. The list often includes the following:

- **Loan or payoff verification statements (can link online accounts)**
- **Bank statements (can link online accounts)**
- **Proof of employment (W-2, recent pay stubs, or two years of 1099 tax returns)**
- **Proof of residency**
- **Proof of graduation**
- **Government-issued ID**

Finally, you'll have to consent to a hard credit pull to confirm your interest rate. You also have the option to refinance with a co-signer, which might help you qualify for a lower rate.

Note: After you submit your application and start the underwriting process, you can lock in your new low rate for up to twenty-eight days before finalizing the loan.

- **Step 5: Consider Underwriting Factors That Impact Loan Approval and Interest Rate**

  Many factors can contribute to loan approval, and each bank has its own criteria. In general, your debt-to-income ratio (DTI) will decide if you get approved, while your credit score and work history will determine your interest rate.

Underwriting Factors:

- **Total student loan amount:** Most banks prefer a lower DTI, usually 2.5 to 1 or lower. So if you've got $250,000 in student debt, you'll ideally want a yearly income of $100,000 or more.

- **Total annual income salary (including any fill-in 1099 income):**

  - W-2 income: A job offer letter might work if you're a new OD graduate, but usually, a three to six month work history is preferred.

  - 1099 income: If you're self-employed, you'll typically need a minimum of one year's worth of 1099 tax forms, but often two years.

- **Total monthly expenses + rent:** Living at home or renting a cheap room could boost your chances of getting approved. The fewer expenses and more

---

income you have, the better your rate will be.

- **Good credit score:** To qualify for decent rates, aim for a credit score of 740 or higher. Lower scores will work with some lenders, but expect a significantly higher rate. A score above 775 will likely snag the best rates. You can check your score for free at CreditSesame.com or CreditKarma.com.

- **Cash reserve:** Some lenders want to see that you have 10–20 percent of your student loan amount in your checking or retirement accounts. This requirement varies among lenders; the idea is they want to ensure you have sufficient cash flow for emergencies and can make your monthly payments. Note that this can be difficult for new graduates, so you might need to save or borrow from family to meet this requirement.

- **Other restrictions:** Certain lenders operate only in specific states, like Texas.

- **Co-signer option:** If approval is challenging, a spouse or family member can co-sign your loan to improve your chances. We generally don't recommend using a co-signer, but if you do, look for a lender that offers co-signer release.

- **Step 6: Sign the Final Documents** Once approved, you'll need to sign the final documents to accept your loan. A three-day rescission period starts when you sign the loan's final disclosure. You can cancel the refinance loan during this period if you change your mind.

- **<u>Step 7: Wait for Loan Payoff</u>** After the three-day rescission period, your new lender will pay off your existing loan or servicer. From then on, your payments will go to the new refinance lender. Keep paying your existing lender until you get confirmation that the process is complete. If you overpay, you'll be refunded.

For any cash bonuses, expect them to be paid out to your account 90–120 days after your loan closes.

7 STEPS HOW TO REFINANCE YOUR STUDENT LOANS

☑ **1) SELECT THE AMOUNT OF LOANS THAT YOU WANT TO REFINANCE.**

☑ **2) GET AT LEAST THREE ONLINE QUICK RATE QUOTES *(SOFT CREDIT PULL)*, THEN SELECT THE BANK WITH THE BEST AND LOWEST RATE *(2-3MINUTES)***

☑ **3) CHOOSE YOUR LOAN DURATION | VARIABLE OR FIXED RATE**

☑ **4) GET ALL YOUR FINANCIAL DOCUMENTS + COMPLETE THE APPLICATION *(HARD CREDIT PULL)***

☑ **5) CONSIDER UNDERWRITING FACTORS THAT IMPACT LOAN APPROVAL AND INTEREST RATE**

☑ **6) SIGN THE FINAL DOCUMENTS**

☑ **7) WAIT FOR THE LOAN PAYOFF**

One of ODs on Finance's crowning achievements is our ability to negotiate the best possible rates and cash-back bonuses with both large and small student loan refinance companies specifically for ODs. Make sure to scan the QR code and bookmark the page for when you start working.

That way, when it's time to refinance, you'll have all the advantages of the lowest rates from all major lenders at your fingertips.

6 Student Loan Strategies You Should Know Before Graduating

(1) Skipping the Grace Period

Federal student loans come with a mandatory six-month grace period that you can't skip, even if you'd like to. However, if you're aiming for any forgiveness program, you'll definitely want this grace period. There is a workaround: consolidating your loans as quickly as possible. Make sure to specify that you wish to consolidate immediately, not at the end of the six-month grace period. It takes four to six weeks to process, but once completed, you can enroll in your Income-Driven Repayment (IDR) program of choice (likely SAVE) and start making 0 percent payments. This tactic essentially earns you six extra IDR-qualifying payments toward any forgiveness program.

(2) Filing a Fourth-Year Tax Return to Maximize IDR Payments

When enrolling in an IDR-based forgiveness program, such as the ten-year Public Service Loan Forgiveness (PSLF) or twenty- to twenty-five-year Total Forgiveness, the objective is to make the smallest payments required. This means making absolutely no extra payments each month. To show your income during the IDR application process, you can use your previous year's tax return.

If you had no income during optometry school but still filed a tax return, the Department of Education will consider you as having a $0 income, thus making your IDR payments $0. If you lack a tax return, you will need to use alternative documentation of income, like pay stubs, which will likely result in higher payments. Therefore, we recommend filing a tax return during your fourth year of school, even if not required.

(3) Counting Residency Toward IDR Payments

If you're completing a one-year residency and foresee a ten-year career in the VA, IHS, or academic non-profit sector, consider enrolling in the ten-year PSLF program. With the relatively low resident salary, your monthly IDR payments, via SAVE, for instance, will probably only be a few hundred dollars. Yet these payments will count toward the 120 qualifying IDR payments needed for forgiveness.

(4) Leveraging Traditional Retirement and HSA Accounts to Lower AGI

Typically, individuals in lower tax brackets benefit more from Roth retirement accounts, as these accounts allow for paying taxes upfront while in a lower bracket. In contrast, traditional retirement accounts defer taxes until withdrawal, often at a time when the individual is in a higher tax bracket. While this model might hold true for most working professionals, including optometrists at the peak of their careers, it's generally not the optimal strategy during periods of low income, such as a residency.

However, the math changes for those enrolled in loan forgiveness programs. For these individuals, making tax-deferred contributions to traditional retirement accounts is often more advantageous. This approach lowers your overall adjustable gross income (AGI), which is the basis for calculating your Income-Driven Repayment (IDR) monthly payments. By reducing your AGI, you effectively lower your monthly loan payments, leaving a greater amount of debt to be forgiven at the end of the ten-year or twenty- to twenty-five-year forgiveness period.

If you're eligible for a tax-deferred Health Savings Account (HSA) in conjunction with a High Deductible Health Plan (HDHP), we strongly recommend contributing the maximum amount allowed to this account. This strategy offers a triple tax advantage: you receive a tax break at the time of your contribution, the funds grow in a tax-sheltered environment, and any withdrawals used for qualified healthcare expenses are tax-free. This approach not only provides immediate tax benefits but also allows for tax-efficient growth and spending, making it an ideal component of a well-rounded financial strategy.

(5) Utilizing Married Filing Separately (MFS) with SAVE Prepayment in a Forgiveness Program

I won't delve too deeply here, as this advanced strategy should be managed in consultation with your CPA and student loan financial advisor. If you're a married borrower aiming to maximize Public Service Loan Forgiveness (PSLF), you may choose to file your taxes as Married Filing Separately (MFS) rather than Married Filing Jointly (MFJ).

Although choosing MFS often results in a higher overall tax burden, it allows you to use only your personal income—not your combined household income—to calculate your Income-Driven Repayment (IDR) payments. For instance, consider a resident optometrist married to a software engineer: filing jointly would significantly inflate their required payments, reducing the amount eligible for forgiveness.

Filing MFS during residency, however, would lower payments and increase the sum to be forgiven. While this strategy might elevate your total taxes paid, the boost in the amount forgiven could more than compensate for the extra tax expense. Note that under the SAVE program, filing MFS doesn't offer an advantage since both spouses' incomes are considered for IDR calculations.

(6) Establishing a Forgiveness Side Fund

Given current federal student loan rules, borrowers should anticipate a hefty tax bill at the end of a twenty to twenty-five year forgiveness term—often around $100,000 for a typical doctor. To prepare for this, we recommend setting aside funds in a separate taxable brokerage account, comprising a balanced mix of low-cost stock index funds and bonds.

(7) Eliminating Consumer Debt and Enhancing Your Credit Score for Student Loan Refinancing

When considering loan refinancing, or any form of lending like home or practice loans, multiple factors come into play, with each bank setting its own qualifying criteria. Your debt-to-income ratio typically governs whether you'll be approved, while your credit score and employment history influence your interest rate. If you have existing consumer debt or a low credit score, now is the time to eliminate that debt and aim to raise your credit score to at least 750.

Summary

For the majority of ODs, **refinancing to a lower rate is often the recommended path**. This forces you to devise a game plan for your student loan payoff, whether that's wiping it out within five years through aggressive payments or channeling extra cash flow toward other financial goals, like practice ownership, by securing a low-interest rate with a longer fifteen-year fixed term.

Optometry students! Whew, that was a long chapter, but you've finally reached the end! We've poured a lot of research and information into this topic because, for most doctors, it's likely the largest financial—and perhaps even personal—stressor. Our aim was to make you aware of all the financial pitfalls, helping you sidestep the common mistakes associated with student debt and providing strategies to tackle it efficiently.

To end this chapter on a high note—yes, I'm using that Hamburger Technique from your clinical methods class—the most important thing is to stay motivated! This journey is one of the most challenging you'll face in your life. Some days, you might find yourself emotionally drained, feeling helpless and reduced to tears in the corner of your exam room. On other days, you might feel like Wonder Woman! Keep tabs on your progress each month. Celebrate the small victories, like paying off each $5,000 or $10,000 increment.

Absolutely take a well-deserved and debt-free vacation once you've cleared your student loans. Lean on the support of colleagues and friends who are in the same boat; their accountability can help keep you on track, especially if you find yourself coveting that shiny new BMW.

You've got this! You made it through optometry school; this is just another hurdle to clear.

Need more help? Check out the **Student Loan Payment | Forgiveness CALCS** for various payment options + forgiveness tax bill etc. to better inform your decision.

Key Takeaways:

- In 2023, the average starting salary for new optometry graduates hovers around $120,000, while the average student debt continues to climb, often surpassing $250,000. In some cases, doctors rack up nearly $350,000 in debt. Given this landscape, it's increasingly vital for optometry students to understand financial pitfalls and to create a robust student loan repayment plan as soon as they begin earning a doctor's salary.

- There are five main strategies for repaying optometry school loans, each with its own set of pros and cons: tuition reimbursement programs, standard federal payment plans, ten-year Public Service Loan Forgiveness (PSLF), twenty- to twenty-five-year Total Federal Loan Forgiveness, and aggressive debt payback through student loan refinancing. It's crucial to identify which route is the best fit for you, both personally and financially.

- Federal repayment plans can get confusing, but don't worry! Typically, during your school exit interview, choosing between SAVE and PAYE is recommended. If you aim for total federal loan forgiveness, SAVE usually results in the lowest total payments over twenty-five years, while PAYE offers a shorter forgiveness term of twenty years. However, if you're considering refinancing your loans or eyeing the ten-year PSLF program, SAVE is your best option.

- For those fortunate optometrists who qualify for the ten-year PSLF program, this is often the most financially savvy choice. Just make sure you meet all the requirements and stick to them for a decade.

- Though we generally don't champion loan forgiveness, we do see three particular scenarios where optometrists might find this option financially beneficial. Most notably, the twenty- to twenty-five-year Total Forgiveness program can be advantageous for those with a high debt-to-income ratio of 2.5:1 or more. While it's not unthinkable for an optometrist earning $100,000 to pay off a whopping $300,000 in student loans, doing so would necessitate an extremely tight budget and could take much longer than five to ten years to accomplish. Exceptions do exist, of course.

- At ODs on Finance, we encourage optometrists to take control of their financial destiny, rather than relying on fluctuating government policies—especially over a twenty-five-year span. With that said, we see twenty- to twenty-five-year Total Loan Forgiveness as a last resort. Optometrists should carefully weigh their long-term financial and career goals before committing to such a lengthy federal loan forgiveness program. The bottom line is, life is unpredictable, and staying in debt for twenty- to twenty-five years could seriously hamper your wealth-building opportunities.

- While we strongly advocate for leveraging lower interest rates to aggressively pay down your loans, we also want to caution you about specific situations where refinancing might not be advisable. These include eligibility for a ten-year PSLF, higher debt-to-income ratios, financially unstable periods, and, most importantly, the potential loss of federal repayment benefits.

- We recommend beginning your refinancing journey with platforms like Splash and Credible, as they collectively cover approximately 90 percent of all refinance lenders. Afterward, obtain one to two additional quotes from other lenders, such as Earnest, SoFi, or Laurel Road. This approach will provide you with a comprehensive view of your personal market rate, based on your unique financial situation, including credit score, debt-to-income ratio, and work history. We regularly share an OD on Finance promo highlighting lenders currently offering the best rates.

- When it comes to refinancing, several factors influence loan approval, each bank having its own criteria. Generally, your debt-to-income ratio will determine your approval status, while your credit score and employment history will impact your interest rate.

- For the majority of optometrists, refinancing to a lower rate is often the best course of action. It compels you to create a strategy for your student loan repayment, whether that involves eradicating it in five years through aggressive payments or allocating extra cash flow toward other financial goals, like practice ownership, by locking in a low interest rate with a fifteen-year fixed term.

CHAPTER 15

PAYING OFF DEBT VS. INVESTING: WHAT SHOULD I DO FIRST? | BY DAT BUI, OD

> Whatever interest rate you have—whether it's a student loan at a 7 percent interest rate or something else—paying off that loan essentially earns you a 7 percent return. This immediate return is much safer than trying to pick stocks or invest in real estate.
> —**Mark Cuban**

Personal finance is called "personal" for a reason: it's as much an art as it is a science, not unlike prescribing glasses. In all seriousness, determining which financial goal to tackle first is often one of the most challenging decisions doctor-investors face. It's a question that has frequently kept me awake at night.

As an optometry student, your financial plan might look relatively straightforward:

(1) **Establish a three- to six-month emergency fund based on expenses, not income.**

(2) **Minimize student loan borrowing.**

(3) **Adhere to a budget while in school.**

(4) **Pay off any high-interest debts, like credit cards.**

(5) **Contribute to a Roth IRA ($6,500 for singles in 2023).**

(6) **Begin repaying student loans to avoid accumulating interest.**

However, as you transition into your role as a doctor, your financial landscape is likely to shift dramatically. While there are numerous financial gurus offering one-size-fits-all, strictly ordered lists of "baby steps" meant to suit everyone, these approaches are often inadequate. Everyone's financial situation is unique, and the complexity varies widely from person to person.

For example, a newly graduated optometrist burdened with massive student loans and high-interest credit card debt will have different priorities than a seasoned OD nearing retirement. Our aim with this chapter is to provide guidelines that will help you critically evaluate your individual financial goals as a doctor and prioritize them based on your unique circumstances—most importantly, your own attitude toward debt and goals.

(1) Define Your Financial Goals

The first step is to think in terms of goals. Make a list of what your personal financial objectives are.

Do you aim to pay off your student loans in one to five years, or are you comfortable stretching it over ten years? Do you plan to buy a home soon, or is renting acceptable for the foreseeable future? Are you looking to open a private practice? Do you hope to start a family sooner rather than later? Do you wish to retire well before the traditional age of sixty-five? Is caring for your elderly parents a priority?

While everyone's goals differ, many doctors might consider these eight general financial objectives:

- Maintain an emergency fund covering three to six months of expenses.
- Eliminate high-interest consumer and/or non-mortgage debt (such as credit cards and student loans).
- Save for retirement.
- Save for a down payment on a house.
- Set aside funds for a private practice (if applicable).
- Save for children's college education (if applicable).
- Pay off your home mortgage.
- Live generously and embrace the life you desire.

Your financial goals should be both motivating and deeply personal. They are the reason you endure an hour-long commute or handle a difficult patient with professionalism. They fuel your repeated "Which is clearer, one or two?" queries, day after day, year after year. No one's ultimate aim is to merely accumulate a million dollars; it's what that million can achieve that genuinely matters.

(2) Multi-Task Multiple Financial Priorities

While we acknowledge the power of intense focus on a single financial objective—such as aggressively paying off student loans or building up a house down payment—it's crucial to manage multiple financial goals simultaneously. Just as you balanced studying for binocular vision and ocular disease finals in school, you should be able to multitask financially.

An optometrist putting off retirement savings for five or ten years while paying down student debt would be ill-advised, given the power of compounding interest.

And if your employer offers a 6 percent match on your 401(k) or IRA contributions, make sure to take advantage of this. It's essentially free money that you shouldn't ignore. Remember, any employer match should be considered part of your salary.

(3) Evaluate Your Risk Tolerance and Debt Attitude

Your personal comfort level with risk should influence whether you focus more on debt repayment or retirement investing. While the math may show that a typical student loan with a 6.8 percent interest rate (or even a refinanced rate of 3.9 percent) may not be as exciting as an S&P 500 index fund yielding a 10 percent annual return, remember that investing carries its own risks.

Paying off a student loan offers a "guaranteed return" of its interest rate, and that can be invaluable depending on your own risk tolerance. Recognizing your comfort level with risk is an essential part of your financial personality as an investor.

"Dat, Aaron, and Chris! Argh, Can You Just Tell Me Where to Start?"

The Optometrist's Step-by-Step Guide

Here's a list of financial steps, current as of 2023, designed to kickstart your financial journey. Remember, these are guidelines and should be tailored to fit your personal situation:

(1) **Establish an emergency fund covering 3-6 months of expenses (not income).**

(2) Contribute to your primary workplace's tax-protected retirement account up to the employer's match.

For example, fund your 401(k), SEP/SIMPLE IRA up to your employer's match.

(3) **Eliminate high-interest debt (above 8 percent). This includes credit card debt and car loans.**

(4) **Invest in tax-protected retirement accounts (at least 10 percent, ideally 20-25 percent once all non-mortgage debt is cleared)**

On a doctor's salary of $120,000, aim to direct at least 5 percent toward your Roth IRA, while also contributing another 10 percent to your workplace 401(k). Do this as you work on paying off your student loans.

(5) **Aggressively pay off all non-mortgage debt between 5-7 percent.**

This should encompass most of your student loans at a 6.8 percent interest rate. Even if you've refinanced to a lower rate around 3-4 percent, consider prioritizing this debt.

(6) **Max Out All Tax-Deferred Retirement Accounts, Such As 401(k)/SEP/SIMPLE IRA ($22,500 for 401(k)) and Roth IRA via Backdoor ($6,500)**

Aim to allocate 20-25 percent of your income toward retirement. If one spouse isn't working, consider a spousal Roth IRA.

(7) **Invest in a Health Savings Account (HSA: Up to $3,850 Single, $7,750 Family) if You Have a High-Deductible Medical Plan**

(8) Invest in a Taxable Brokerage Account (Long-term Capital Gains Tax ~15 percent; No Limits)

Choose index funds for short-term financial goals (less than 5 years) or for additional retirement savings. For example, save for a down payment on a house if applicable, aiming for a 10-20 percent down payment.

(9) Save for Your Child's College Fund (If Applicable)

Consider tax-deferred accounts like state 529 plans, which have limits that vary by state ($235K-$529K).

This usually includes most home mortgages and private practice business loans.

(10) Further invest in taxable accounts (such as index stock funds) or real estate rental properties.

(11) Pay off loans with interest rates between 3 and 5 percent.

(12) Eliminate low-interest loans (below 3 percent).

The goal is to be debt-free as you approach retirement or achieve financial freedom.

(13) Enjoy the life you've worked hard for: spend wisely and give generously.

Financial Tip

If you're an optometrist with aspirations of owning your own practice in the next three to five years, maintaining a healthy cash reserve should be your top priority. Banks generally require that you have 7–10 percent of your business loan in cash reserves, with a minimum of $25,000. In such cases, it may be wise to first build up this capital.

One approach could be refinancing your student loans to a longer term, like ten years. While this might result in a higher interest rate, your monthly payments would be lower, freeing up cash for your business venture. Alternatively, you could stick with the federal income-driven repayment like SAVE to accumulate the necessary funds.

Once your practice is up and running—which will likely drastically increase your owner's salary—you can then refocus on paying off your student loans. Surprisingly, as long as the practice projected profit/loss shows a positive cash flow, having a large student loan debt is NOT a major factor nowadays.

Summary

We often advise our doctor-investors not to carry any debt, including a home mortgage, into retirement. Losing the safety net of a steady income poses significant financial risks.

However, remember that these are just guidelines. It's completely acceptable if you prefer to focus solely on eliminating student loans because you despise debt.

At times, you might concentrate more on saving for retirement or a house down payment. Your goals will likely evolve; some years you may focus on attacking student debt, while other years you may shift toward bolstering your retirement funds.

The key is to create a game plan and get started!

Key Takeaways:

- Personal finance is unique to each individual. Define your financial objectives, such as paying off student loans, buying a home, or planning for retirement. Your goals should be deeply personal and motivating.

- While focusing on one financial goal can be powerful, it's essential to manage multiple objectives simultaneously. For instance, while paying off student debt, don't neglect retirement savings, especially if there's an employer match.

- Risk tolerance and debt attitude. Your comfort with risk should guide your financial decisions. While investing might offer higher returns, paying off a loan provides a guaranteed return equivalent to its interest rate.

- Flexible financial planning: While guidelines suggest not carrying debt into retirement, it's okay to adjust based on personal preferences. Your financial strategy might evolve over time, but the crucial part is to have a plan and initiate it.

CHAPTER 16:

YOUR FIRST JOB—APPLYING, INTERVIEWING, AND CONTRACT REVIEW AND NEGOTIATIONS | BY CHRIS LOPEZ, OD

> In business, you don't get what you deserve, you
> get what you negotiate.
> **—Chester L. Karrass**

Applying for jobs starts with comprehensive supportive material, mainly an updated resume and/or curriculum vitae. Use these tools to showcase your educational background and clinical experiences, as well as soft skills like patient care and communication. Highlight relevant rotations and specialized skill sets when applying to career positions using the various optometric career search portals online.

Create your free employee profile and get in front of thousands of potential employers at Careers.ODsonFinance.com	

During the interview process, be prepared to demonstrate your clinical acumen and interpersonal skills. Stay ready to showcase hands-on exhibitions of optometric techniques in a real-world clinical setting.

As mentioned in chapter 11, *"Career Prepping During Optometry School,"* leave a positive impression on employers by flipping the script and emphasizing what you can do for the employer, not what the employer can do for you.

Reviewing contracts can be tedious, challenging, and confusing. However, the contract review and negotiation phases of the career-search journey are arguably the most crucial steps in the entire job search process. This could set you up for huge financial success early on in your career, or it could keep you stuck at an office out of fear of breaching your contract.

There are numerous contractual elements to look out for when reviewing a contract, such as the non-compete agreement, termination notice, and exclusion/devotion clause, amongst others. The non-compete should be reasonable and may vary dramatically based on setting and geography. There is a movement to render non-competes void, and it has already taken effect in several states, with more states expected to join.

Termination notices indicate the length of time that either an employee or an employer will give the other party ahead of the contractual agreement coming to an end. Notices are usually thirty to ninety days.

Exclusion, or devotion, clauses tend to describe an employee agreeing to devote their entire professional time to an employer and render said associate unable to perform fill-in services if desired. This may not matter to some of our colleagues, but it does to those who would like the opportunity to moonlight in other offices.

Of course, there are more elements in a contract that warrant adequate understanding.

Consider reaching out to a consultant or attorney who works with ODs on reviewing and negotiating contracts. A few hundred dollars could gain you thousands in compensation and spare you from accepting a poor opportunity.

The final step in securing a dream optometrist position is negotiating the offer. Negotiating is not easy. In fact, it's an extremely difficult skill to master. However, the payoff can be tremendous. To be clear, job gratification is not entirely dependent on income. Unfortunately, many colleagues who forego negotiating end up feeling undervalued, which may lead to anger and resentment. *That* is why negotiating is so crucial. You are more likely to be happy in your workplace if you feel valued and appropriately compensated for your time and efforts.

The key to negotiation is simple. ASK. Sure, asking for higher pay can seem uncomfortable, but is it really less troublesome than feeling short-changed? At the same time, it would be a mistake to ask for more money simply because you think you deserve it. Yet, if you can demonstrate your value to the employer and illustrate what you can do to improve the practice (and profitability), the hiring party may be more willing to offer some improvements to the contract.

In short, do not shy away from this final stage in the career search journey. Crushing a contract negotiation can lead to extraordinary job satisfaction. Exude confidence, know your worth, demonstrate your value to the practice and employer, and ask for what you want. Negotiate like a pro.

Takeaways

- Begin your job application with an updated resume or CV, highlighting your education, clinical experiences, and soft skills. Utilize optometric career search portals, like ODs on Finance Careers, to apply for relevant positions.

- During interviews, showcase your clinical expertise and interpersonal abilities. Focus on what you can offer the employer, emphasizing your contributions rather than what you expect in return.

- Thoroughly review job contracts, paying attention to elements like non-compete agreements, termination notices, and exclusion clauses. Given the significance of these contracts in shaping your career, consider consulting with professionals experienced in reviewing and negotiating optometrist contracts.

- Negotiating your job offer is vital for job satisfaction and feeling valued. Approach negotiations confidently, demonstrating your worth and contributions to the potential employer. Remember, the key is to ask and negotiate effectively to ensure you're adequately compensated for your skills and efforts.

CHAPTER 17

PRACTICE OWNERSHIP—IS IT RIGHT FOR YOU? | BY AARON NEUFELD, OD

Entrepreneurship is living a few years of your life like most people won't so you can spend the rest of your life like most people can't.
—Warren G. Tracy

Chances are high that at some point along your optometry school journey, you will think about practice ownership. Even for those dead set on working in industry or academia, the question of business ownership does cross their mind. And with good reason!

Remembering back to chapter 11, the highest average income levels historically belong to practice owners. However, it is important to note that with ownership's unlimited ceiling, there exists a double-edged sword. We've known plenty of owners that eclipse $500,000 or even $1,000,000 in take-home earnings each year from their practices, but on the flipside, we also know owners that barely take home $70,000 annually.

The reason for this huge delta in earning potential can be blamed on certain metrics to an extent (cost of goods, low revenue per patient, real estate costs, dependency on vision plan reimbursement, etc.), but ultimately, all these metrics fall on the owner. Specifically the owner's drive, grit, and business acumen.

I've had the opportunity to own successful practices for much of my career, but more importantly I've had the privilege of learning from some of the best mentors in the practice ownership space. Through our conversations we've found the following points to be a great litmus test for whether the practice ownership dive fits your life journey.

(I) **Answer Yes to the 5 Key Questions**

(II) **Are You Taking the Red or Blue Pill?**

(III) **Understand How Ownership Fits Into the Grand Scheme**

(IV) **Create Your Business Plan and Understand It**

(V) **Realize Your Why**

Let's dive into each point.

(I) Answer Yes to the 5 Key Questions

Whenever I talk with an OD or budding OD interested in practice ownership, I bring up the 5 Key Questions. It's important to spend some time reflecting on yourself when going through these questions. Ideally, your answers to each question should be a solid "yes," and your answers may change over the course of your career.

(1) Can You Take Multiple Responsibilities?

Ownership means you are no longer just a doctor—you are now a manager, accountant, marketer, buyer, and staffer.

While you may have individuals you eventually delegate to these roles, you must still be able to understand and perform multiple responsibilities in order for your business to truly run effectively.

(2) Can You Make Tough Interpersonal Decisions?

Despite personal connections you make, the nature of business may and most likely will force you to cut ties with individuals. Two of the hardest decisions I ever made in my practice were firing a patient and a staff member. Emotions run high, and stress can run even higher—but you must be ready to pull the trigger if needed.

(3) Can You Stomach Periods of Negativity?

Regardless of the positive metrics you may see regarding income potential, periods of negativity are inevitable with every business. Industry changes may cause a downswing in patients, a power outage may cause a week of lost revenue, or a break-in may cause a loss of inventory. It is an owner's responsibility to deal with these periods of negativity and make sure his or her staff and patients are covered.

(4) Can You Take Ownership of Everything?

One thing every business owner needs to understand is that any mistake that occurs in the business is ultimately their fault.

It may sound harsh, but think about it—every aspect of your business is a reflection of you. Is there a mistake in the optical regarding a patient's glasses? You should have trained the appropriate staff better. Was there a lack of medical reimbursement that led to a cash flow crunch? You should have brought in the right services to prevent that from happening. An owner who understands that every fault that occurs is their own, even if another individual commits the fault, is an owner who will be successful.

(5) Can You Eat It?

Things happen. And those things will, at some point, hit the fan. That's life as a business owner. If you sweat the little things, you miss the big picture. If every bad thing that occurs in your practice leads you to a spiral of depression, then you're in for a hellish existence. As an owner of a successful practice, it's important to accept a problem, deal with it, and then move on as quickly as possible.

(II) Are You Taking The Blue Pill Or The Red Pill?

If you've ever seen the 1999 sci-fi film *The Matrix*, you probably remember one of the most important scenes in which Lawrence Fishbourne's character Morpheus asks Keanu Reeve's character Neo to choose between a red pill and blue pill.

While the movie's connotation for the red pill and blue pill represents the difference between a simulation and reality, our analogous take here is the difference between starting a practice from scratch (colloquially known as **starting cold** in the optometry sphere) versus **buying out** an existing practice (complete purchase) or **buying into** an existing practice (becoming an equity partner).

It's important to understand the differences that come between the red pill and blue pill. Starting cold enables you to customize your business completely to your vision; however, it will take, on average, about two to three years to reach profitability. This will mean a couple of years of grinding (with plenty of mistakes) while moonlighting to make ends meet. Starting cold is not for the faint of heart, and on paper it may seem like a very difficult uphill battle. However, it is important to remember that every business has to start at some point!

Has cold starting a practice crossed your mind? ODs on Finance has developed the <u>Cold Start Accelerator,</u> which provides all the resources, guidance, and funding needed to start a practice cold at the lowest possible cost. Scan the QR code and bookmark this page!	

Buying (in or out) an existing practice may allow for positive cash flow from day one, but it is not without significant challenges. You'll be dealing with an established system, which will most likely be resistant to changes you will need to make. Additionally, all the underlying issues and bad habits of this established system will now be your own liabilities and responsibilities. It will be your job to set the ship sailing in the right direction, all while dealing with a loan amount that is probably much higher than what you would take for starting a practice cold.

(III) Understand How Ownership Fits into the Grand Scheme

Practice ownership is much more than a full time job, and often requires many hours of work and limited time off (especially in the early years). It is important to factor in how this will affect your personal life. If you are planning to get married or start a family, will ownership allow you to still spend adequate time with your spouse and/or children? If you are planning to travel or pursue further education, will ownership allow you the time to do so? These are all questions that must be answered.

(IV) Create Your Business Plan and Understand It

While creating a business plan and the actual ins and outs of practice ownership/management are far beyond the scope of this book, it is important that you at least have a rough business plan written out for your potential dream practice.

Start thinking about a few things:

1) **How are you paying for this thing?** Consider financing options and how these will play into your bottom line (how much money will be left over after all expenses are considered).

2) **How will you allocate funds?** Build-outs, equipment, frames, staff, and even chairs all come at a cost, and money doesn't grow on trees. Plan out your budget for the essentials to get your practice going.

3) **How are you making money?** Getting patients through your door is not a guarantee that you will be profitable. There must be a plan of action on how you will bring in revenue through a combination of professional services and materials sold. Will you offer specialty services? What insurances will you take?

It doesn't hurt to have your business plan on paper. The exercise will help you start thinking about the future. Need some help writing a business plan? Check out this guide that we wrote to help you: odsonfinance.com/the-optometrists-guide-to-writing-a-business-plan.

(V) Realize Your Why

Your why is vital. If you don't have a reason or passion for why you are owning a practice, you'll be on a quick path to burning out and resentment of your profession.

Realize your *why*.

Also realize that everyone's why is different. Your *why* might be to treat dry eye at the highest level.

It might be to serve as many patients as possible in an underprivileged community. Or it might be to make millions of dollars a year. Each *why* is completely valid, so the key is to understand what it is and to pursue it in both an ethical and honest manner.

As you close this chapter on practice ownership, remember that the journey of an optometrist is filled with choices, challenges, and opportunities. The path to ownership is not just about financial gains or business acumen; it's about passion, purpose, and the impact you wish to make in the world of optometry. Your *why* will be your guiding light, illuminating the way even in the face of adversity. Embrace the lessons, cherish the experiences, and always keep your vision clear. As future leaders in optometry, you have the power to shape the future of eye care. So dream big, stay committed, and let your passion for the profession guide you to greatness.

Key Takeaways:

- Ownership has the potential to create a lot more income than employment. However, it also has the capability of doing the opposite.

- Being an owner is dynamic and difficult—reflect on whether you can answer yes to the 5 Key Questions before pursuing ownership.

- Write out a basic business plan for your practice so you can start getting the gears going on what you want out of your future practice.

- Understand your unique *why* behind being an owner and how ownership will factor into your future lifestyle.

If practice ownership is of interest to you, make sure to check out our Practice Owner website for resources that will help you thrive!	

CHAPTER 18:

FINDING SUCCESS AND BEATING THE NORM: A REAL-LIFE CROSS-COMPARISON | BY AARON NEUFELD, OD

> Success is to be measured not so much by the
> position that one has reached in life as by the
> obstacles which he has overcome.
> **—Booker T. Washington**

Warren Buffet. Oprah Winfrey. Lebron James.

What do these three individuals have in common? Besides being billionaires, not much else. And that's the beauty of it. There are many roads to financial success. However, unfortunately, the most common and easily understood routes are highlighted as the "only way." Modern thought concurs that a billionaire needs to start a fledgling tech company from their parents' garage, when in reality, none of the three billionaires in the preceding paragraph took that route. The same goes for optometry. You don't necessarily need to own twenty practices or invest in the next volatile cryptocurrency to achieve financial success.

With average annual incomes of $130,000 for employed associate optometrists and $250,000 for practice owner optometrists, many individuals think that optometry can provide a good enough or comfortable life but nothing spectacular. Furthermore, the student loan debt burden, as well as other life obstacles such as mortgage payments and family expenses, lead prospective ODs to think that financial freedom and success lie well into their presbyopic futures.

But that's not necessarily true.

In this chapter we will profile four real-life optometrists who achieved financial success early in their careers. They all took unique routes that vary greatly. The numbers are real, and the stories are real, because they're four ODs that are either authors of this book or very close friends/colleagues to the authors of this book.

Sure, these accounts are purely anecdotal. However, all of these individuals are regular ODs at the end of the day—just like you will be. They went to the same schools, took the same boards, and shared the same passion for saving vision. So read the following with this in mind: they might be outliers, but *you* surely can be as well.

Dr. A

Dr. A decided early on that practice ownership was not for him. After a couple years of soul-searching while living in California, he decided to find a long-term salaried position that would offer competitive benefits, a high salary, schedule flexibility,(and the ability to be in a leadership role. The compensation lands around $200,000 annually, although the patient care is a bit dull—mainly refracting nit-picky engineers. The schedule flexibility enables Dr. A to work 3.5 days a week and be "off" the other half of the week. Except Dr. A is a bit ambitious and fills his 2.5 days with two projects: (1) building a special interest company and (2) investing in real estate which he actively manages. He also occasionally helps emerging health tech companies on consulting gigs and fills in at local primary care offices.

By year five, Dr. A has also eliminated all his student loan debt and has built a sizable nest egg in his Vanguard portfolio, consisting of his 401k/Roth IRA/taxable accounts, which generate an average of 8 percent per year ($25,000).

A breakdown of Dr. A's total annual income at year 5 can be viewed below:	
Salaried position	$200,000 + benefits
Special interest company	$150,000
Residential real estate	$35,000 (+ $72,000 in equity building)
Consulting/fill-in	$55,000
Vanguard portfolio income	$25,000
TOTAL REALIZED + UNREALIZED INCOME	$537,000

From the above graphic, we can see that Dr. A pulls over half a million dollars in income each year and has a net worth of north of $1 million. And he's doing this all without owning a practice!

Dr. B

Dr. B hails from sunny Southern California. However, he chooses to eschew the life of beaches and palm trees for the frigid tundra known as the rural Midwest. Being financially savvy and also aware of his value, Dr. B, just like Dr. A, chooses not to own a practice but rather to be a fill-in doctor. He understands that a high volume of patients in need of care and practices in need of a doctor to see these patients gives him extraordinary leverage powers. Thus, Dr. B is able to swing rates of more than $1,000 per diem.

But Dr. B doesn't keep all this information to himself. He offers it to ODs searching for jobs as well as OD employers searching for employee ODs through consulting. In fact, he's built enough of a reputation that he does additional consulting and speaking for industry on the same topics. He also has an equity stake in Dr. A's special interest company.

Oh yeah, and remember how he lives in the frigid Midwest? His house is paid off, which allows him to retain much more of his annual income. His nest egg, a Fidelity portfolio consisting of 401k/simple IRA/taxable accounts continues to grow yearly.

Here is a breakdown of Dr. B's total annual income at year 5:	
Fill-in optometry	$220,000
Consulting—individuals	$100,000
Consulting/speaking—industry	$20,000
Fidelity annual portfolio income	$20,000
TOTAL REALIZED + UNREALIZED INCOME	$360,000

Dr. B shows a healthy and hefty income, and all without owning a practice. He also has no debt, which ensures he maximizes his retention of his income. Once again, the mold of the average associate income of $130,000 annually is broken.

Dr. C

Dr. C ended up in California in a similar vicinity as Dr. A. However, Dr. C realized early on that he couldn't work for someone. Thus, he began his search for an existing practice to purchase. He eventually found himself buying out an owner of a full-scope practice that was looking to retire.

Although the first year of practice ownership was rough, each consecutive year, Dr. C was able to improve and grow the practice by restructuring finances, adding services, and marketing nonstop.

He saw his annual income from the practice go from $140,000 in year one to $410,000 in year five. Along the way, he was able to purchase the building that houses his practice and adjacent businesses. Furthermore, he landed a few lecturing and advisory gigs related to practice management/ownership. He also co-founded and co-owns the special interest company with Dr. A.

Lastly, he has built a solid nest egg of Roth IRA/taxable accounts in his Vanguard portfolio and owns a home in which he rents out an in-law unit.

Dr. C's total annual income breakdown at year 5 is listed below:	
Owners salary + distributions	$410,000
Speaking/advisory roles	$100,000
Commercial real estate	$12,000 (+ $102,000)
Special interest company	$150,000
Fidelity portfolio income	$30,000
TOTAL REALIZED + UNREALIZED INCOME	$804,000

Dr. D

Dr. D is also a West Coast optometrist, but more importantly, a serial entrepreneur. Upon graduation, she teamed up with her husband (who is also an OD) to open a cold start private practice as well as take a lucrative corporate sublease. Although the cold start will take a couple years to yield profitability, the corporate sublease allows both of them to live comfortably, pay off loans, and buy real estate. By year three, both are generating substantial net income.

From day one of her career, Dr. D has committed all of her extra income to purchasing residential real estate properties out of state in more affordable areas. She utilizes the familiar strategy of buying distressed properties at a bargain, renovating them, putting them up for rent, and then utilizing cash-out refinancing (a more advanced concept in real estate investing—read our site for more info!) to recoup her initial investment dollars to buy more properties. By year five, she has amassed ten properties with significant cash flow.

Along the way she has contributed to her Schwab portfolio consisting of Roth IRA/taxable accounts and has owned and significantly paid down the mortgage on her home.

Dr. D's total annual income breakdown at year 5 is listed below:	
Owner's salary + distributions— private practice	$200,000
Owner's salary + distributions— corp. sublease	$300,000
Residential real estate cashflow (+ equity building)	$120,000 (+ $200,000)
Special interest company	$50,000
Schwab portfolio income	$30,000
TOTAL REALIZED + UNREALIZED INCOME	$900,000

Realize Your Potential

As an aspiring doctor, it is easy to pigeonhole yourself with a fixed ceiling prematurely. Salary surveys commonly cited represent the median, and those who have trouble with money tend to be more vocal, because the big earners are too busy, well, earning!

With your optometry degree, you are giving yourself a unique set of skills that can differentiate you from the average individual.

Even as a starting associate, you are already at an income level that is nearly double the national average.

Realizing that this "disposable income" is not really "disposable" and can be used as an opportunity for wealth building is key. Also realizing that optometry is not as black-and-white as working a nine-to-five, Monday to Friday is key as well. Manage your time to prioritize your passions, and be prudent with your income.

Want a supplement to your associate position at a corporate office? Start a side hustle selling on Etsy.

Want a change from your position in academia? Start consulting and giving lectures on the side.

Want to be your own boss? Search and network to find a practice for sale, or start one cold, and talk to banks for financing. NO ONE is stopping you.

Stop Comparing and Start Doing

And at the end of the day, do realize that comparison really is the thief of joy. While the earlier part of this chapter profiled various ways of attaining outlier success in optometry—you can still live a perfect life and have a fulfilling career with a totally median and average salary of $150,000 per year—especially if your debts are paid off, you are well insured, you are investing for the future, and most importantly, you are happy.

A lower income level does not mean that you will become less financially successful, nor does a high income level mean that you will become more financially successful. What truly matters is how you approach your available funds day to day.

Investing behavior and debt reduction over the span of years have the power to be far more valuable than an extra $100 per diem. Where you choose to live and how much you pay to live also factor in. Remember Dr. B from our doctor profiles? He may have the lowest income, but his paid-off house is three times as large as each of the California-based doctors', and he also has two acres of land. Perspective is a large plus-powered lens when looking at the effects of money and how to stretch its efficacy to achieve the lifestyle you want.

Key Takeaways:

- There are many ways to build wealth. Be creative with how you generate your income, and remember that your time is worth a lot and will continue to be worth more as you gain experience.

- The sky's the limit for income potential both in and out of the profession.

- Become the outlier by doing and taking charge of your own financial destiny.

CONCLUSION

OUR PHILOSOPHY + WORDS OF WISDOM | BY DAT, AARON & CHRIS

Congratulations, you've nearly made it to the end of this book! If you decided to skip to this chapter or only read this chapter, that's fine too. Our goal is to summarize the important points we highlighted in detail in our previous chapters and solidify the most important concepts when it comes to finances for the student optometrist.

In this chapter you will find fifteen statements of advice from various parts of these books. We encourage you to memorize them, but more so understand what they mean and how to apply them to your life now and when you become a doctor.

(1) **Understand why money should not be your primary motivator as a doctor:** Remember to follow your passion. If you don't like what you do, then you're on a slippery slope to burnout and misery. Let your motivator be your passion for your craft, and the money will follow.

(2) **Always seek to buy assets, not liabilities:** Remember the IEAL machine. While most of society stays on the liabilities/expenses side, you know that staying on the assets/income side will take patience and willpower but will ultimately lead to a better life.

(3) **Understand how to save money and limit loans in optometry school while also reducing the risk of catastrophe:** Great money habits start when you are in school. That means understanding your finances, taking control of your budget, and properly insuring yourself.

Once you hit the "real world," these behaviors are already ingrained, allowing you the ability to pursue financial freedom.

(4) Practice work/life balance to prevent burnout: Do you know what's worse than getting burned out as a practicing clinician? Getting burned out before you even start practicing. Prioritize work/life balance and self-care early on so it becomes an ongoing habit you carry into your career.

(5) Understand if residency is right for you: Some of the most successful optometrists did not do a residency, and some of the most successful optometrists have done a residency and swear by it. So what's the right choice? The choice that's best for you. Weigh whether you value jumping into the fold with a full paycheck vs. getting additional specialized training with a smaller paycheck for a year to choose the path that is right for you.

(6) Choose the right practice modality based on passion and financial implications: For some, their destined career path may occur the second they step foot in their first job. For others, it may require bouncing around for years. Regardless, finding a modality that is fulfilling comes down to a balance of what you want to spend your time on and whether you are being compensated properly for that time spent.

(7) Have a step-by-step career checklist for each year of school: Failing to plan is planning to fail. Make sure that you follow a step-by-step career checklist similar to the one outlined in this book. This will not only properly prepare you for your career but also put you on the path to financial freedom.

(8) **Know basic investment principles and how to prepare for retirement:** Investing is boring and actually not very complicated. It boils down to time horizon and balancing risk. The simple answer to building wealth that millions of Americans have embraced? Invest in a low-cost broad-market index fund like the S&P 500 Index. Automate your investing for a time interval that works best for you. Utilize tax-advantaged retirement vehicles such as a 401(k)/403(b), Roth IRA, and HSA first, and then place the rest in a taxable brokerage account.

(9) **Understand your student loans and how to tackle them:** Student loans are often cited as the most daunting aspect of graduating from optometry school. Looming monthly payments for the foreseeable future can be discouraging; however, having a firm understanding of what path you will take (refinancing, 10-year PSLF, 20-25-year Total Federal Forgiveness) and your timeline to conquer your debt will give you peace of mind and a light at the end of the tunnel.

(10) **Understand loan payoff vs. investing:** While student loans have a guaranteed negative "return," the stock market (or any other investment) does not. You may be debt averse or risk averse, which means you focus on knocking out loans first before heavily investing, or you may be a risk taker—which means you will probably want to delve into investing before paying off loans. Regardless of what personality you have, the key is to start early, find a happy balance, and realize that no one can predict the future.

(11) Insure yourself against catastrophe: Accidents and tragedies are an unfortunate part of our world. Make sure you are protected against them—ensure that you have proper malpractice insurance, buy your own occupation disability insurance, and if you have dependents, purchase term life insurance.

(12) Taxes affect everything: Everything from income to investments get taxed. In fact, one of your biggest expenses in life will be taxes. Prioritize tax-advantaged retirement accounts and work with a CPA on strategies to minimize your tax burden as you continue to increase your income.

(13) Choose your career path wisely: Each modality of practice offers unique opportunities in how we push our profession forward and serve our patients. Alongside this, each modality has different income potentials that are confounded by geographical regionality. Learn as much as you can about what you want to do, and make sure that your chosen career path will serve you both from a financial satisfaction and clinician satisfaction standpoint.

(14) Be wary of snakes and snake oil: Unfortunately, the nature of finance and the general perception of doctors having a lack of knowledge in finance opens our profession up to attack by unscrupulous and dishonest individuals looking to capitalize on naivety. Most often they will offer you an investment that is too good to be true or some sort of whole/variable life insurance. They won't be able to answer hard questions, and they'll use smoke and mirrors to sell their products. Your knowledge from this book will help you sniff them out.

Remember to always refer to trusted sources of information when it comes to finance by jumping on our website: odsonfinance.com.

(15) Remember that you have the potential to be very successful: Optometry is a blue ocean. As an employed OD, you have the option to make a good living. As an owner, you have an endless ceiling of earning potential. That coupled with smart debt management and disciplined investing will quickly put you on the path to financial freedom. That financial freedom will allow you an even deeper appreciation for our profession. Because that's what it's all about: serving our patients, taking care of our families, and living a life of purpose.

EPILOGUE

We often get asked why we started ODs on Finance. Why did we give up the standard nine-to-five optometry routine for constant travel to events, content creation, hosting CE summits, and student outreach? The truth lies in our passion for our profession, which at a deeper level stems from our passion for all of our colleagues to achieve financial success.

Here's the thing: financial education is not covered much or at all in optometry school—and that makes sense. You pay big money to learn about optometry-related topics like diagnosing glaucoma and fitting scleral lenses rather than learning about a 401(k) plan or disability insurance. **However, financial prudence is key to our profession's continual survival.**

As our profession goes to war with insurance providers, technological disruptors, and massive conglomerates hellbent on turning us into a commodity (rather than a service), being financially fit becomes more and more important. Having our finances in check allows us to have the freedom to not choose to take a certain corporate job from a company that actively works against our profession. As practice owners, it allows us to not take certain vision plans or burn ourselves out seeing too many patients for too little pay.

Financial education allows us to spot con artists looking to take our hard-earned money, such as the sleazy whole life insurance salesman and the off-putting "financial specialist OD," as well as pointing out poor speculative investments

The truth is that money makes the world spin. As the great collective of philosophers better known as the Wu-Tang Clan stated: "Cash rules everything around me." However with the knowledge you possess after reading this book, you will realize that YOU rule cash that is around you and, therefore, your professional destiny.

There is a constant looming doubt that low incomes and heavy debt loads will eventually cause an end to our profession as we know it. *You are the force that stands in the way of those doubts. Armed with your newfound financial education, you can contribute to keeping our profession salient and robust so we can best do what we set out to do as optometrists—save vision and care for our patients.*

WELCOME TO THE ODS ON FINANCE COMMUNITY

Congratulations on a rare achievement among optometrists: successfully navigating a financial book. Dat, Aaron, and Chris crafted this guide with the hope that you'll not only gain immediate insights but also chart a course for your future financial endeavors. Our aim is for you to feel inspired and empowered to achieve the financial success you deserve. As you delve deeper into the concepts presented, you'll find yourself mastering the many facets of financial life, from earning and saving to investing, spending, and giving.

Now in the time in the book, where we entrust you with our personal email address. Over the years, many have reached out for guidance, feedback, comments, and questions either via email or Facebook Messenger, or in real life at meetings. We are happy to say that we have always replied to each member of the ODoF Community, whether there to give them some life advice, sometimes pointing them to a relevant blog post and at other times connecting them with professionals. On the ODs on Finance website, under the Recommended Resources, we've curated a list of trusted professionals, from student loan refinancing, business financing, and practice resources to attorneys and accountants. They come highly recommended by a vast community of optometrists. Additionally, our extensive library offers an OD's Financial Guide, updated annually to reflect tax codes and legislative changes.

ODs on Finance Website	Practice Owner Website	FaceBook Community
https://odsonfinance.com	https://practice.odsonfinance.com/	https://www.facebook.com/groups/ODsonFinance

Our Facebook group is a treasure trove of resources. Here, you can pose questions and join thousands of your peers on a journey toward financial freedom, both personally and professionally.

If you ever find yourself in need of guidance or simply want to reach out, email us at Admin@ODsonFinance.com. We take pride in our personal touch and aim to respond to every email.

Now, as we've shared our email with you, we hope you'll do the same. We promise not to overwhelm you with emails, and you can always opt out. By signing up, you'll gain access to our free monthly newsletter, crucial financial updates pertinent to our profession, free CE events, and a plethora of financial tools.

Sign Up Now for Our Newsletter!	 https://odsonfinance.com/newsletter-2/

Lastly, we have a small request. The more reviews a book garners, the more visibility it gets on Amazon. To help disseminate this crucial information to more students like you, please consider leaving a review. We've journeyed through pivotal financial decisions you'll face during school and the initial years of your career. We've touched upon the most vital aspects of a doctor's financial literacy. Now, it's time to bring what you've learned to life. Remember, you're not alone in this journey. Along with the entire ODs on Finance community, Dat and Aaron will be right beside you every step of the way.

Cheers to Financial Freedom,

Dat Bui & Aaron Neufeld
Co-Founders
www.ODsonFinance.com

ABOUT THE AUTHORS

Dr. Dat Bui, O.D (Co-Founder)

Dr. Dat Bui graduated from the Southern California College of Optometry (SCCO/MBKU) in Fullerton, CA. He practices optometry on the Apple Campus in the heart of Silicon Valley. With a keen interest in ocular disease and healthcare technology, he began his career with over $230,000 in student loan debt. Through strategic budgeting, personal finance, and investing, he cleared this debt in just four and a half years. Dr. Bui is a staunch advocate for passive index funding, with a portion of his portfolio dedicated to technology stocks. He also manages a large residential five-plex in the Bay Area, CA. As a co-founder of ODs on Finance, optometry's premier personal finance platform, he co-authored the Amazon best-seller, *The Optometrist's Guide to Financial Freedom.* Alongside this, he consults for technology companies, aiming to guide new doctors and high-earning professionals toward wealth and financial independence.

Dr. Aaron Neufeld, O.D (Co-Founder)

Dr. Aaron Neufeld graduated from the Southern College of Optometry in Memphis, TN. He now lives in the Bay Area, CA, where he owns two full-scope private practices, with an emphasis in specialty contact lenses and myopia management. He began his career with $160,000 in student loan debt and eliminated it (along with investing) in two years. He has a passion for both index funds and commercial real estate investing.

Beyond his clinical work, Dr. Neufeld co-founded ODs on Finance, the leading finance and investing platform for optometrists and optometry students. He has penned over thirty articles for optometry publications and co-authored the Amazon best-seller, *The Optometrist's Guide to Financial Freedom*. Additionally, he's an esteemed speaker and consultant on industry topics, having delivered multiple COPE-approved CE lectures on myopia management, practice management, and marketing.

Dr. Chris Lopez, O.D (Career Director)

Dr. Christopher Lopez graduated summa cum laude from the University of Houston College of Optometry. Originally from Southern California, he now calls Wisconsin home, living there with his family. Chris is on the path to practice ownership. His clinical focus lies in ocular disease and specialty contact lenses. Beyond his clinical responsibilities, Dr. Lopez contributes to various optometry journals and travels nationwide to deliver COPE-approved CE lectures. He's deeply committed to assisting optometry students and young ODs in their job search journey. Chris serves as the Director of Career Services for ODs on Finance.

Made in the USA
Las Vegas, NV
14 December 2023

82768853R00177